The Anxious Attachment Recovery Handbook

Proven Techniques to Build Trust
in Relationships, Develop Meaningful
Connections & Enhance Inner Security to
Emotionally Thrive

Tanya Dransfield

Xone Publishing

© 2024 by Tanya Dransfield, Xone Publishing

All rights reserved. No part of this publication may be reproduced, distributed, or transmitted in any form or by any means, including photocopying, recording, or other electronic or mechanical methods, without the prior written permission of the publisher, except for brief quotations embodied in critical reviews and certain other noncommercial uses permitted by copyright law.

This publication is designed to provide accurate and authoritative information in regard to the subject matter covered. It is sold with the understanding that neither the author nor the publisher is engaged in rendering legal, investment, accounting or other professional services. While the publisher and author have used their best efforts in preparing this book, they make no representations or warranties with respect to the accuracy or completeness of the contents of this book and specifically disclaim any implied warranties of merchantability or fitness for a particular purpose. No warranty may be created or extended by sales representatives or written sales materials. The advice and strategies contained herein may not be suitable for your situation. You should consult with a professional when appropriate. Neither the publisher nor the author shall be liable for any loss of profit or any other commercial damages, including but not limited to special, incidental, consequential, personal, or other damages.

Moral rights

Tanya Dransfield and Xone Publishing assert the moral right to be identified as the author and publisher of this work.

External content

Tanya Dransfield or Xone Publishing is not responsible for the persistence or accuracy of URLs for external or third-party Internet Websites referred to in this publication and does not guarantee that any content on such Websites is, or will remain, accurate or appropriate.

Designation

Designations used by companies to distinguish their products are often claimed as trademarks. All brand names and product names used in this book and on its cover are trade names, service marks, trademarks, and registered trademarks of their respective owners. The publishers and the book are not associated with any product or vendor mentioned in this book. None of the companies referenced within the book have endorsed the book.

Contents

Foreword		VII
Introduction		IX
1.	Understanding Anxious Attachment	1
2.	The Impact of Anxious Attachment on Relationships	16
3.	Communication Strategies for Anxious Attachers	34
4.	Building Self-Esteem and Personal Identity	50
5.	Practical Exercises for Managing Anxiety in Attachments	65
6.	Healing from Past Relationship Trauma	83
7.	Navigating Relationships with Avoidant and Disorganized Types	101
8.	Advanced Strategies for Relationship Success	120
9.	Special Considerations in Anxious Attachment	137
10.	Empowering Your Journey Toward Secure Attachment	156

Conclusion 168
Your 2 Bonus Gifts 173
About the author 177
References 179

Foreword

There can be little doubt that anxiety is one of the most prevalent psychological issues affecting the world today. And while anxiety comes in many guises, The 'Anxious Attachment Recovery Handbook' tackles one of the most devastating forms. In exploring this problematic topic, Tanya demonstrates her considerable knowledge and first-class skill set, offering the reader a genuine opportunity to tackle this issue 'head on. However, this should be no surprise, as Tanya has clocked up more than two decades working and teaching in the field of psychotherapy, including teaching and training the author of this preface.

Whether you're suffering directly or looking to understand what may be happening to a loved one, Tanya's book will undoubtedly be of great value and assistance in understanding and working with this complex emotional and psychological issue.

Andrew Mercer BA (Hons), DHP (adv.), CJP, PGCE. Life Change Therapy - Clinical Psychotherapy. Registered with the College of Medicine.

Introduction

Have you ever felt like your relationships seem to hit the same stumbling blocks no matter how hard you try? Perhaps you find yourself constantly worried about being too much or too little for someone, always on edge about how they feel toward you. If these feelings sound familiar, you might be experiencing what's known as anxious attachment.

Anxious attachment can make you feel like you're on an emotional roller coaster. It is predominantly characterized by a hunger for closeness paired with a fear of abandonment. This might show up as needing frequent reassurance from partners, friends, or family members, or maybe you find yourself interpreting neutral situations as negative without real cause. These are not just patterns but cries from deep within for security and understanding.

My journey into the realms of anxious attachment began in my own early life. I navigated through a maze of strained relationships and self-doubt until I found a path that led me to deeper self-awareness and healthier interactions. This book is born from my work as a psychotherapist, professional research, and personal battles, crafted to guide you from uncertainty to confidence and connection.

In ***The Anxious Attachment Recovery Handbook***, our goal is to understand the underpinnings of anxious attachment and transform our relationships into the supportive, loving structures we all deserve. This book dissects the anxious mind and applies real, actionable strategies to address our fears and foster genuine intimacy. Plus, it is filled with self-help tips, techniques, and practical exercises, so you can create your own unique strategy for overcoming, thriving, and transforming anxious attachment.

What sets this guide apart is its blend of personal stories, up-to-date research, practical self-assessment, and self-reflection exercises at the end of each chapter that respect your unique life context. Whether you're single, in a relationship, or navigating the complexities of family and friendships, each chapter is tailored to help you recognize unhealthy patterns and equip you with the tools to create lasting change.

Also included are your **2 bonus gifts: Transformational Audio Tracks** professionally designed by me, the author. These tracks work subconsciously using carefully crafted hypno-suggestions to build self-esteem, boost confidence, and promote emotional resilience. They will enhance the effectiveness of the tips and strategies in this book.

- **8-Hour Sleep Transformation Track for Building Self-Esteem, Confidence, and Overcoming Anxious Attachment**

- **7-Minute Power Booster Track for Daily Confidence Boost and Emotional Stability**

You can easily download these tracks to your phone or laptop, making them accessible whenever needed. Just follow the link or scan the QR code found on page 173

You, the reader, are the reason this book exists. Whether you're a young adult just exploring the dating world, a parent seeking to build stronger bonds with your children, or anyone in between, this book is your companion. It acknowledges the diverse experiences we bring to our relationships and offers a compassionate, informed path forward.

As we embark on this journey together, remember that this book is more than just a source of information—it's a call to action. Engage with the exercises, reflect on the insights, and allow yourself to be open to the transformation that awaits.

Let's start this journey of self-discovery with optimism and courage, knowing that the keys to more secure and fulfilling relationships are within our reach. Together, we will explore these pages and take brave steps toward a more connected and confident you.

I want you to know that you are not alone. I, too, struggled with a disorganized attachment style. The techniques and strategies in this book are not just theoretical—they are the same powerful yet simple tools that helped me transform my life and relationships. If I can do it, I know you can too. As I would say to my clients, "They work if you work them." So, let's embark on this journey of growth together.

Chapter One

Understanding Anxious Attachment

Do you recall the last time you felt a pang of anxiety when your text message went unanswered for a few hours or when someone you care about seemed slightly less enthusiastic than usual? These moments can feel like subtle shifts in the wind, but for someone with an anxious attachment style, they might feel more like hurricanes disrupting their emotional balance. Anxious attachment is a term that touches on the profound impact of our earliest experiences with closeness and connection, shaping how we respond to relationships throughout our lives. This chapter will guide you through understanding this complex attachment style, providing clarity and insight into why you feel the way you do and how those feelings affect your interactions with others.

1.1 Defining Anxious Attachment: More Than Just Clinginess

Often misunderstood merely as clinginess, anxious attachment unfolds as a fear-based state within relationships, characterized by a hypersensitivity to relational cues and a chronic need for reassurance. This condition stems not from a place of over-dependence but from deep-seated fears of abandonment and rejection. Imagine consistently feeling that your value in your relationships hangs by a thread, one that could snap with the slightest sign of disinterest or disapproval from those you care about. This fear drives individuals to vigilantly seek signs of affirmation or threats of withdrawal, often misinterpreting or exaggerating the significance of relational dynamics.

Contrasting this with other attachment styles illuminates its unique challenges. Unlike securely attached individuals who typically exhibit confidence and stability in relationships, those with anxious attachment often struggle with trust and self-worth, leading to turbulence and insecurity. Compared to avoidant attachment, where individuals maintain emotional distance and self-sufficiency, anxious attachers crave closeness and are highly invested in their relationships, sometimes overwhelmingly so. Disorganized attachment, marked by erratic responses due to unresolved traumas, also differs significantly, as it lacks the consistent pattern of intense relational focus found in anxious attachment.

The emotional experience of anxious attachment is intense and consuming. Fears of abandonment can transform what are objectively minor issues into emotional calamities. These fears are not baseless but are exaggerated responses rooted in real feelings of vulnerability and a deep desire for connection. The emotional whirlwind can include profound joy at perceived closeness and devastating despair at the slightest hint of rejection. This heightened emotional sensitivity can strain relationships, leading to cycles of conflict and reconciliation. Often, the anxious attacher's behavior, driven by their need for security, can inadvertently push others away, reinforcing their fears of abandonment and perpetuating a cycle of distress and repair.

Understanding this attachment style's impact on relationships is crucial. It's not just about the internal turmoil the individual experiences but also about how these patterns affect their partners, friends, and family. Relationships involving anxious attachment often face challenges such as constant misunderstandings, emotional highs and lows, and an ongoing need to address and soothe insecurities. These dynamics can be exhausting for all involved, making recognizing and addressing the underlying issues essential for healthier, more stable relationships.

Recognizing the signs and understanding the roots of anxious attachment can empower you to transform your approach to relationships, turning patterns of fear into acts of love and assurance. As we explore these themes, remember that awareness is the first step toward change. By understanding your attachment style, you can begin to foster healthier, more fulfilling relationships built on mutual trust and understanding rather than fear and uncertainty.

1.2 The Science Behind Attachment: Why Your Brain Clings to Others

Understanding why we form attachments and why they can sometimes lead to anxiety requires a dive into the fascinating interplay between our psychological theories and biological mechanisms. The roots of attachment theory are traced back to the seminal work of John Bowlby and Mary Ainsworth, who revolutionized how we perceive human development. Through his observations, Bowlby posited that attachment was an evolutionary mechanism vital for survival. Infants are biologically programmed to form attachments with caregivers as a means to secure safety and sustenance. Ainsworth expanded on this by identifying the different styles of attachment through her famous "Strange Situation" assessments, which observed how children reacted when separated from, and then reunited with, their caregivers. This foundational work is crucial as it underscores the importance of early relationships in shaping our approach to adult relationships.

Neurological underpinnings suggest our brains are wired to connect. Two critical areas, the amygdala and the prefrontal cortex, play pivotal roles in this process. The amygdala, often referred to as the brain's alarm system, processes emotional reactions and is particularly attuned to fear-based responses. For those with an anxious attachment style, the amygdala may elicit heightened vigilance and sensitivity to threats in the relational sphere, interpreting even minor signs of disengagement as potential dangers. This can lead to the persistent unease and need for reassurance seen in anxious attachment. On the other hand, the prefrontal cortex, which governs reasoning and decision-making, might struggle to regulate these emotional responses, leading to overwhelming anxiety that can disrupt relationships.

Neurotransmitters also play a critical role in connecting and responding to others. Oxytocin, sometimes called the 'love hormone,' is integral in emotional bonding and increases feelings of closeness and security. In contrast, cortisol, the 'stress hormone,' can become elevated under constant anxiety, destabilizing the sense of security and potentially exacerbating feelings of attachment anxiety. An imbalance between these chemicals can create a challenging dynamic for those with an anxious attachment style, wherein the body's stress response is frequently activated, making calm and reasoned responses to relationship stresses more difficult.

The evolutionary perspective on anxious attachment suggests that, in our ancestral past, being hyper-alert to social cues and changes in interpersonal dynamics might have had survival benefits. In environments where threats were frequent, detecting early signs of conflict or withdrawal could facilitate proactive behaviors to mend social bonds or alert the group to potential dangers. Today, although we are far removed from these ancestral environments, these evolutionary imprints can persist, manifesting as heightened sensitivity to relational dynamics in our modern, often less dangerous world.

This scientific framework helps to explain why individuals with an anxious attachment style experience love and fear so intensely and why their brains might cling to others in ways that are both profound and, at times, profoundly challenging. Understanding these mechanisms is not just an academic exercise; it provides a compassionate lens through which to view our struggles with attachment, paving the way for targeted strategies that address both the psychological and biological roots of anxiety in relationships.

1.3 From Childhood to Adulthood: Tracing the Roots of Anxiety in Relationships

Childhood lays the foundation of our emotional blueprint, shaping how we perceive and react in adult relationships. Our interactions with our caregivers are pivotal, as they set the initial patterns that can lead to secure or anxious attachments. When these early relationships become marked by inconsistency or unpredictability, the seeds of anxious attachment are sown. Imagine a young child whose parent is affectionate and attentive one day but distant or dismissive the next. This child learns to be constantly vigilant and hyper-aware of the caregiver's moods and behaviors, adapting their own behaviors to secure love and attention. This vigilance often evolves into an acute sensitivity to relational cues that can later manifest as anxiety in adult relationships.

The influence of these early experiences extends into adolescence, a developmental stage where peer relationships become central to emotional growth. For those with foundational anxious attachments, adolescence can be a minefield. Each social interaction has the potential for rejection or acceptance, and the stakes feel immeasurably high. Here, the patterns ingrained in childhood are either reinforced or challenged. An adolescent might gravitate toward friendships or romantic relationships that mirror the inconsistency they're accustomed to, reinforcing their anxious attachment style. Alternatively, positive interactions with peers—who are consistent, reliable, and supportive—can offer a corrective experience, planting the seeds for healthier relationships in the future.

When transitioning into adult romantic relationships, these early attachment patterns often resurface. For adults with an anxious attachment style, the romantic partner may become the focus of intense scrutiny and high expectations, similar to those once directed toward their caregivers. Common triggers such as minor disagreements, changes in routine, or even normal periods of individual activity can be misinterpreted as signs of waning interest or affection. These misinterpretations can provoke profound anxiety and lead to behaviors that inadvertently push partners away, such as messaging incessantly or demanding reassurance, thus repeating the cycle of fretting and reconciliation observed in their early relationships.

Consider the case of Anna, a woman in her thirties who frequently found herself in tumultuous relationships. As a child, Anna's father was loving but deeply unpredictable, his attention often shifting based on his mood. As Anna grew older, she was drawn to partners who displayed similar behavior patterns—charming and affectionate one moment, withdrawn the next. Each time her partners pulled away, it reignited her deep-seated fear of abandonment, leading to panicked attempts to restore closeness. These relationships, invariably characterized by intense emotional highs and lows, mirrored the instability of her early experiences with her father. Through therapy, Anna began to understand how her childhood experiences had shaped her expectations of love and connection. This new knowledge allowing her to work toward forming healthier, more stable relationships that broke her historical pattern.

Understanding the trajectory from childhood through to adult relationships highlights the profound influence of early experiences on attachment styles. It also underscores the importance of addressing these root causes. By recognizing and exploring early patterns, we can begin to understand our anxieties in relationships, paving the way for healing and growth. This deep dive into our attachment history is not just about uncovering pain; it's about opening a doorway to transformative change that can lead to more fulfilling and less fearful relationships.

1.4 Anxious Attachment and Self-Esteem: The Inner Link

The dance between anxious attachment and self-esteem is intricate and profound. At the heart of many anxieties that fuel attachment fears lies a deep-seated sense of unworthiness. This feeling of not being enough can pervade every thought and interaction, shaping how we perceive ourselves and how we believe others perceive us. For those grappling with anxious attachment, this often manifests as a relentless quest for reassurance and approval. An internal narrative drives anxious attachers to earn their place and stay in every relationship.

This interconnection is crucial to understand because it reveals that anxious attachment is not just about how we relate to others but fundamentally about how we relate to ourselves. Low self-esteem does not simply surface; it is a culmination of internalized beliefs, often rooted in early experiences where an individual felt they could not consistently secure affection or approval just by being themselves. These experiences teach them that love is conditional and must be constantly earned, translating into adult relationships as a continuous need for validation. This need is a response to the underlying fear that perhaps, at their core, they are not enough to hold someone's love or even their attention without extra effort.

The implications of this are far-reaching. When people believe they are inherently lacking, they are likely to set lower expectations for their relationships and accept less than they deserve, perpetuating a cycle of dissatisfaction and insecurity. In some cases, this might lead to choosing partners who reinforce their negative self-beliefs and selecting relationships that are unstable or undervalued because they align with their self-image. Each relationship failure or rejection then confirms their fears, embedding the feelings of unworthiness even deeper.

Breaking this cycle requires more than just understanding the patterns—it demands self-perception reconstruction. Initiating this change involves cultivating a sense of self-worth independent of external validation. It's about learning to appreciate ourselves, recognizing personal strengths, and accepting imperfections not as flaws but as facets of our individuality. This shift can significantly mitigate the anxieties associated with attachment, as the individual no longer looks solely to others to define their value.

One practical approach is targeted self-esteem-building exercises, such as journaling achievements and positive qualities or engaging in therapy modalities that focus on cognitive restructuring. These activities help reframe thoughts from critical self-assessments to supportive self-acknowledgment. Another strategy is the practice of self-compassion, which encourages an individual to treat themselves with the same kindness and understanding they would offer a good friend. This practice can be especially powerful for those with anxious attachment, as it directly addresses the harsh self-judgment that often accompanies their relational fears.

Moreover, setting boundaries in relationships can play a critical role in enhancing self-esteem. By defining and asserting our needs and expectations in relationships, we send a message to ourselves as much as to others that we are worthy of respect and consideration. This can alter our interactions with others and gradually rebuild our internal belief systems about our worth.

As we explore these strategies further in subsequent chapters, the focus will remain on practical, actionable steps that individuals can take to understand and manage their attachment anxieties and fundamentally transform how they view themselves. The journey toward healing is not just about altering how we engage in relationships with others but about changing our relationship with ourselves. By addressing the root of the issue—low self-esteem—there is a profound opportunity to change the entire dynamic of our interpersonal relationships and significantly reduce the anxiety that often accompanies attachment issues.

Improving self-esteem can provide a more stable foundation for developing healthier attachments. As self-worth grows, the overwhelming need for external reassurance diminishes, allowing for relationships based on mutual respect and genuine connection rather than fear and insecurity. This transformation is not instantaneous, nor is it always linear, but it is both possible and profoundly life changing. Through the thoughtful application of the strategies we will discuss, we can begin to see ourselves in a new light, paving the way for more secure and fulfilling relationships.

1.5 Recognizing Anxious Behaviors in Daily Interactions

In the fabric of daily life, the behaviors characteristic of anxious attachment can often manifest subtly, yet they profoundly influence our sense of well-being and relationship dynamics. Recognizing these behaviors is the first critical step toward managing them effectively. Commonly, individuals with anxious attachment find themselves engaging in constant texting or communication with their partner. This behavior isn't just about staying connected; it's a way to continually confirm the relationship's stability and the partner's affection. They might also scrutinize their partner's words and actions, reading deeply into what might be casual remarks or routine behaviors. This over-analysis often stems from a fear of underlying issues or potential abandonment.

Beyond communication, these behaviors can extend to how individuals interpret their partner's social interactions or career demands. For someone with an anxious attachment, a partner's regular social outing or a late night spent at work can trigger profound anxiety. They might worry whether their partner's social interactions could lead to emotional or physical infidelity or whether time spent on career demands indicates shifting priorities away from the relationship. It's the uncertainty and perceived lack of control over these external factors that can lead to heightened anxiety.

Physically, this state of constant vigilance and worry can take a toll. Many with anxious attachment experience physical symptoms of anxiety, particularly concerning their relationships. These can range from insomnia, where the mind races at night over details of the relationship, to more acute stress responses like stomach issues or headaches. Recognizing these physical manifestations is crucial as they serve as indicators that anxious thoughts are not just an emotional background noise but are exerting a tangible impact on physical health.

Self-monitoring techniques can be invaluable in managing and eventually mitigating these responses. One effective method is the practice of mindfulness, where we learn to observe our thoughts and feelings without judgment. This practice can help us identify when our thoughts are spiraling into anxious patterns. Another technique is setting clear and realistic expectations for communication. For instance, agreeing on a reasonable frequency of communication with a partner can help prevent the compulsion to send constant messages. Additionally, keeping a journal can be a powerful tool. By documenting instances when anxiety arises in response to specific triggers, we can begin to see patterns and better understand the situations or behaviors that ignite our fears.

These self-monitoring strategies help recognize anxious behaviors and lay the groundwork for developing healthier emotional responses. They are about creating a space between the immediate emotional reaction and the action taken, allowing for more deliberate, thoughtful responses that align with our true needs and desires. This shift is crucial for moving toward more secure attachment behaviors where we feel confident and valued in our relationships without the constant need for reassurance.

As we move forward, remember that the path to changing deep-seated attachment patterns is gradual and requires patience and persistence. The techniques discussed here are not quick fixes but are part of a broader strategy to cultivate a healthy, secure relationship approach. The goal is to foster a sense of security within ourselves that stands independent of external validation. This inner security not only enhances personal well-being but also fundamentally transforms the nature of our relationships, making them more balanced, fulfilling, and resilient to the complexities of life.

Self-Assessment and Reflection Exercises for Chapter 1: Understanding Anxious Attachment

1. Reflect on Early Attachment Influences:

- Exercise: Think about your early childhood experiences with your primary caregivers. What three words best describe these relationships?
  - Action: Identify one way these early experiences might affect your current relationships. Reflect on how this insight can help you understand your behaviors and feelings.

2. Identify Current Relationship Patterns:

- Exercise: Recall a recent situation where you felt anxious in a relationship. What was your initial reaction?

- Action: Write down one alternative response you could try next time. Consider how this new response might change the outcome of similar situations.

3. Understand Your Triggers:

   - Exercise: List three common situations that make you feel anxious in relationships.
   - Action: Choose one trigger and write a calming technique you can use when it happens. Practice this technique and note any changes in your reactions.

4. Assess Attachment Styles:

   - Exercise: Identify which attachment style you most relate to (anxious, avoidant, secure).
   - Action: Write one small step you can take to move towards a more secure attachment style. Reflect on the benefits this change could bring to your relationships.

5. Create an Action Plan:

Exercise: Set a specific goal for improving your attachment style. For example, "I will practice deep breathing once daily when I feel anxious."

- Action: Decide a timeframe (e.g., one month) to achieve this goal and track your progress. Reflect on the impact of this goal on your overall well-being.

6. Overall Reflection:

- Exercise: Choose one key takeaway from this chapter.

- Action: Write down how you will apply this takeaway in your daily life starting today. Consider the potential positive changes this application could bring.

Chapter Two

The Impact of Anxious Attachment on Relationships

Imagine standing on the edge of a cliff, the ocean waves crashing below, and your partner's hand is the only thing holding you back from falling. This image might evoke a sense of thrill and a profound fear of what might happen if that hand lets go. For those grappling with anxious attachment, this scenario can metaphorically resemble their romantic relationships—a constant fear of the fall, paradoxically coupled with a longing to dive into the depths of intimacy and connection. In this chapter, we delve into how anxious attachment molds the dynamics of romantic relationships, often leading to a dance of dependency, misunderstandings, and emotional turmoil, yet also holding the potential for profound growth and deeper bonding if navigated with awareness and mutual effort.

2.1 Anxious Attachment in Romantic Relationships: A Deep Dive

Dependency Dynamics

In the landscape of love and intimacy, anxious attachment can often skew the balance toward dependency, creating relationships where one partner may rely excessively on the other for emotional support and validation. This dependency is not about mere preference for companionship but a compelling need, where the anxious partner's emotional well-being seems almost tethered to their significant other. Such dynamics can strain the relationship, as the weight of one's emotional needs might overwhelm the other partner. The anxious individual often fears that their emotional intensity might drive the partner away, yet feels powerless to contain it. This worry creates a cycle where the need for reassurance can become a relentless pursuit, paradoxically increasing the very insecurity it seeks to soothe.

The roots of such dependency often lie in the core beliefs of individuals with anxious attachment, where self-worth is intricately linked to how their partners perceive and respond to them. Finding yourself in this pattern is like looking into a mirror and seeing yourself through your partner's eyes. The reflection is constantly shifting, unstable, and impossible to pin down, leading to a perpetual emotional flux. Recognizing this pattern is the first step toward recalibration, where we begin to find our emotional footing not in the hands of another but within the stable ground of self-understanding and self-compassion.

Impact on Intimacy

Intimacy, while sincerely sought by those with anxious attachment, often becomes the very arena where their fears play out. The closeness they crave seems laced with risks—of being seen too deeply and, perhaps, of being found wanting. This fear can manifest in behaviors such as jealousy, constant seeking of reassurance, or even smothering—the overwhelming desire to merge with the partner, erasing the boundaries that healthy relationships require. Often rooted in the fear of losing the relationship, these actions can ironically push the partner away, creating the feared abandonment scenario.

Intimacy requires vulnerability, a state that can feel incredibly threatening to someone whose attachment style is woven with threads of anxiety and fear. The paradox here is evident: the more one tries to secure the bond through controlling or demanding behaviors, the more strained the relationship becomes. The path to healthier intimacy involves embracing vulnerability not as a threat but as a gateway to genuine connection. It means letting go of the reins of control just enough to allow the relationship to breathe, find its own pace, and grow in mutually enriching rather than restrictive ways.

Coping Mechanisms for Partners

Navigating a relationship with someone who has an anxious attachment style requires understanding, patience, and a clear set of boundaries. For the non-anxious partner, this might mean learning to provide consistent reassurance without enabling dependency. It's a delicate balance—offering support without becoming the sole pillar on which the anxious partner leans. Setting healthy boundaries is crucial; the partners should communicate clearly and compassionately. For instance, agreeing on times to discuss relationship concerns rather than allowing them to infiltrate every interaction can help manage the intensity.

Moreover, the non-anxious partner can encourage and support their loved one in seeking individual therapy or joining support groups, where they can work on understanding and managing their attachment style.

These strategies can help reduce the pressure on the relationship and empower the anxious partner to take active steps toward self-reliance and emotional resilience.

Transformative Approaches

For couples within which one or both partners have an anxious attachment style, transforming the relationship into a secure base can be a profound journey. This transformation can involve engaging in couples therapy, where guided discussions can help resolve misunderstandings and build a deeper understanding of each other's emotional landscapes. Communication techniques such as active listening, validating each other's feelings, and learning to express needs and fears without blame can also significantly reshape the relationship dynamics.

Moreover, couples can adopt mutual understanding as a cornerstone of their relationship. This might involve regularly setting aside time to share personal fears and aspirations, not as a forum for reassurance but as a space for genuine connection. When shared with trust and openness, these moments can significantly strengthen the bond, turning the relationship into a true partnership where both individuals feel valued, understood, and securely connected.

In exploring these dynamics and strategies, the aim is not just to manage the symptoms of anxious attachment but to foster an environment where love can flourish unencumbered by fear. It is about building a relationship that feels less like clutching at each other on a cliff edge and more like walking hand in hand, secure in the knowledge that the ground beneath is solid and that each step forward is taken together.

2.2 How Anxious Attachment Influences Friendships

Friendships, often seen as less complex than romantic relationships, can nonetheless become intricate labyrinths for those with anxious attachment styles. Imagine yourself in a situation where a friend postpones a long-awaited meetup. While many might shrug it off as a simple scheduling conflict, someone with an anxious attachment could spiral into a distressing analysis of potential rejection or loss. The fear of abandonment and the hypersensitivity to friends' actions and comments can manifest in friendships as an overwhelming need for constant reassurance, a tendency to cling, or a susceptibility to perceive indifference where none exists. These reactions strain friendships and lead to a self-fulfilling prophecy where the fear of losing friends might push them away.

Addressing these challenges begins with self-awareness—recognizing these patterns is the first step toward change. It's important to understand that these fears stem from deep-seated insecurities and past experiences rather than the reality of your current friendships. Adjusting expectations plays a crucial role here. Setting realistic, clear expectations for yourself and your friends can alleviate some of the pressures that come with anxious attachment. For example, understanding that friends have their own lives and that their affection for you is not solely measured by their availability can help reframe your perceptions. Open communication about your attachment needs can also be transformative. It doesn't mean demanding more attention or reassurance but rather explaining your feelings and working together to find a balance that respects your needs and those of your friends.

The role of broader social networks is essential in providing a buffer against the intensity of these dynamics. Diversifying your social interactions can reduce the pressure on any single friendship to fulfill all your emotional needs, which is particularly beneficial for those with anxious attachment. Engaging in group activities, cultivating casual acquaintances, or participating in community events can expand your social circle and provide a sense of security and belonging that isn't overly reliant on close friendships. This approach alleviates the pressure on your close friendships, enriches your social life, and boosts your confidence in social settings.

Furthermore, friendships can be a powerful healing tool, offering a safe space to develop healthier attachment behaviors. Unlike romantic relationships, which can sometimes feel like high-stakes environments to those with anxious attachments, friendships can offer a more relaxed context to practice trust and open communication. For instance, gradually opening up about your fears and vulnerabilities in a friendship can reinforce your understanding that relationships can be stable and supportive, even when they allow for independence and separateness.

Over time, these positive experiences can contribute significantly to building your self-esteem and reducing your relationship anxiety, creating a virtuous cycle where secure attachment in friendships helps foster the same in romantic relationships. In nurturing these dynamics, it's critical to focus on quality over quantity in friendships, seeking out and maintaining relationships with individuals who understand and respect your attachment style and are willing to support you on your path to secure attachment. These friendships, characterized by mutual respect and understanding, can become a cornerstone of your emotional support system, helping you to internalize new, healthier ways of relating to others that can eventually translate into other areas of your life.

2.3 Navigating Anxious Attachment at Work

In professional environments, the interplay between personal emotional tendencies and professional demands can be particularly challenging for individuals with anxious attachment styles. At work, where performance and feedback are constantly scrutinized, the fear of criticism or failure can loom large, coloring interactions and influencing job performance. For someone with anxious attachment, a simple request for a report or a casually made comment about their work can spiral into internal narratives fraught with doubts and fears about their competence and worth.

This anxiety isn't just about the fear of not being good enough; it extends to how these perceived shortcomings might affect an anxious attacher's standing within the team or their relationships with supervisors. The workplace becomes an arena where the stakes feel perpetually high, and every interaction is a potential test. Such pressure can hinder performance, as the focus shifts from doing the job well to an excessive preoccupation with how others perceive their work. This shift affects the individual's work and can strain professional relationships, as colleagues and supervisors may feel puzzled by the anxious individual's need for reassurance or their sensitivity to feedback.

Addressing these challenges begins with fostering clear and open communication. For someone grappling with anxious attachment, learning to seek clarification can be a game changer. Instead of stewing in uncertainty and doubt about an offhand remark or a vaguely worded email, directly asking what the interaction meant can dispel misconceptions and alleviate unwarranted fears. Furthermore, setting clear expectations with one's supervisor about feedback and progress updates can also provide a structured framework that feels more secure. Regular feedback sessions, rather than sporadic or impromptu critiques, allow the individual to prepare and process the information in a less emotionally charged setting, making the feedback more constructive and less intimidating.

Establishing and maintaining healthy boundaries at work is crucial in managing anxious attachment. These boundaries help define the limits of what is personally acceptable and professionally expected, creating a safe space where individuals can function effectively. For instance, it might involve setting limits on checking work emails outside of office hours or communicating our capacity when new tasks are assigned. Such boundaries ensure that work demands do not overwhelm personal capacities and that professional relationships can be based on mutual respect and understanding rather than dependency and fear of disapproval.

Moreover, embracing professional challenges as opportunities for personal growth can significantly alter the perception of workplace interactions. Instead of viewing challenging projects or roles as potential threats, reframe them as opportunities to learn new skills or enhance your professional capabilities. This perspective shift reduces the fear of possible failure and encourages a more proactive and positive approach to professional tasks. Additionally, practicing secure attachment behaviors in a professional setting, such as trusting in our abilities, seeking support when necessary, and valuing constructive criticism as a tool for growth, can reinforce personal development and boost professional confidence.

Navigating anxious attachment in the workplace involves a delicate balance of self-awareness, communication, boundary setting, and a proactive personal and professional growth approach. By transforming how we interact with the professional environment, it is possible to enhance job performance and cultivate healthier and more resilient professional relationships. These changes can lead to a more fulfilling and less anxiety-driven work life, where challenges are met with confidence and a sense of security rather than fear and uncertainty.

2.4 The Interplay Between Different Attachment Styles

When you begin to understand the mosaic of human relationships, you quickly realize that attachment styles are crucial in shaping how interactions unfold. Imagine a dance floor where everyone has a unique style of dancing—some are cautious and maintain a considerable distance, while others prefer a close and constant touch. Much like this dance, relationships involve navigating various attachment styles, each bringing its own rhythm and challenges. The dynamics between an anxiously attached individual and a partner who might be avoidant or securely attached are particularly complex, requiring a nuanced understanding and a thoughtful approach to harmonize these differences.

The interplay between an anxious and an avoidant partner often resembles a chase, where the anxious partner's need for closeness unwittingly triggers the avoidant partner's need for space, setting a cycle of pursuit and withdrawal into motion. On the other hand, the interaction between an anxious and a secure partner might look different; secure partners generally offer the reassurance and consistency anxious individuals crave, but even they can be overwhelmed by the intensity and constant need for validation if not understood and managed effectively. Recognizing these dynamics is pivotal for transforming the relationship into a source of mutual growth and support.

Effective communication is vital in bridging these differences. It involves more than just discussing day-to-day activities; it requires partners to share their deeper fears, needs, and expectations. For instance, if you're anxiously attached, explaining to your partner how certain behaviors get interpreted as signs of distancing can open up a dialogue about each other's perceptions and reactions. Understanding that the avoidant partner's need for space might be perceived as rejection can help them communicate their actions better, allowing them to reassure their partner of their commitment even as they take time for themselves. This kind of transparency can prevent misunderstandings and provide both partners with insights into how to support each other better.

It's important to note that the avoidant attachment type presents in a couple of ways, such as 'fearful avoidant' and 'dismissive-avoidant.' Fearful avoidant individuals, more commonly known as the disorganized attachment style, often experience a mix of anxious and avoidant tendencies, craving closeness but fearing it simultaneously, leading to a contradictory and often unpredictable approach to relationships. Dismissive avoidant individuals tend to downplay the importance of relationships and often distance themselves emotionally. While these styles are relevant and interconnected, the scope of this book focuses on anxious attachment and its unique challenges.

Adapting to your partner's attachment style doesn't mean losing your emotional identity or suppressing your needs; instead, it's about creating a relationship environment where both partners can express their styles and needs without fear of judgment or reprisal. It might mean setting clear expectations about time spent together and apart and finding a balance that respects the need for closeness and independence. It also involves developing coping strategies tailored to each partner's triggers. For example, if an avoidant partner needs space after an argument, pre-agreeing on a timeout period can give them the space they need without triggering anxiety in the anxious partner, who might otherwise interpret this as abandonment.

Let's consider a case study that illustrates these principles in action. Sarah, who identifies with an anxious attachment style, and Tom, who leans toward an avoidant style, frequently find themselves at odds in their relationship. Sarah felt insecure and neglected when Tom pulled away, and Tom felt suffocated by Sarah's constant need for affirmation. Through therapy, they learned to articulate their needs and set up a 'relationship contract' that included agreed-upon times for solitude, together time, and regular 'relationship check-ins' where they could express their feelings in a safe space. Over time, these strategies helped them better understand each other and foster a relationship that catered to their needs without compromising their emotional health.

Understanding and adapting to different attachment styles isn't just about preventing conflict; it's about enriching the relationship. It allows both partners to feel understood and valued, learn from each other, and create a dynamic and resilient partnership. This adaptation requires patience, empathy, and, often, a willingness to step outside our comfort zones. But the rewards—a relationship built on understanding, respect, and mutual support—are worth the effort. As you navigate these waters, remember that the goal is not to change who you are or to change your partner fundamentally but to evolve together in ways that honor both of your attachment styles, fostering a deeper, more meaningful connection. Naturally, this leads to a more secure bond.

2.5 Managing Relationship Dynamics When Both Partners Are Anxious

When both partners in a relationship exhibit anxious attachment styles, they often find themselves in a unique emotional ecosystem where their actions and reactions are intensely magnified. This shared sensitivity can lead to a relationship where both partners are acutely aware of each other's moods and behaviors, interpreting them through a lens of anxiety and insecurity. In such dynamics, a simple offhand comment or a slight behavior change can be perceived as an alarm signal, triggering a cascade of emotional reactions that can challenge the relationship's stability.

Managing this landscape requires a delicate balance of self-awareness and mutual understanding. One effective strategy is for partners to take turns in giving emotional support. This approach ensures that both partners' needs are met and prevents any one partner from becoming the sole emotional anchor, which can be exhausting and unsustainable in the long run. Learning to self-soothe is another crucial skill for both individuals. Developing personal coping strategies such as mindfulness, deep breathing exercises, or engaging in individual hobbies can help each partner manage their anxiety independently, reducing the overall emotional intensity within the relationship.

Creating a supportive relationship environment is essential for couples dealing with dual anxious attachments. This can be achieved by establishing routines encouraging connection and communication, such as regular 'check-ins' where partners can share their feelings and concerns without judgment. Engaging in shared therapeutic activities, such as couples' yoga or joint therapy sessions, can also enhance mutual understanding and foster a sense of teamwork in managing attachment styles. These shared activities provide a dual benefit: they offer a space for emotional connection and serve as a practical framework within which both partners can work on building a more secure attachment together.

Stories of successful couples who have navigated this dynamic often highlight the importance of open communication and professional guidance. For instance, consider the story of Elena and Mark, both of whom presented with anxious attachment styles. Their relationship was initially a roller coaster of emotional highs and lows, with each partner constantly seeking reassurance and fearing abandonment. However, through therapy, Elena and Mark learned to understand and respect their triggers and devised personal and joint strategies to manage their anxieties. They established rules around communication, explicitly asking for space when needed and offering reassurance when one felt insecure. Over time, these strategies helped them develop a stronger, more balanced relationship that supported both of their emotional needs.

These narratives serve as a testament to the potential for transformation and offer practical blueprints for couples embarking on similar paths. They underscore the possibility of growth and improvement when both partners are committed to understanding their emotional patterns and working together toward a healthier, more secure relationship.

In wrapping up this exploration of dual anxious attachments, it's clear that such relationships, while challenging, hold profound opportunities for growth. When harnessed with awareness and mutual support, each partner's sensitivity can transform a potentially volatile dynamic into a deeply empathetic, understanding partnership. As we transition from understanding these internal dynamics to exploring external influences in the next chapter, remember that the journey toward secure attachment, however complex, is filled with moments of meaningful connection and mutual growth, offering a roadmap for surviving relationship challenges and thriving within them.

Self-Assessment and Reflection Exercises for Chapter 2: The Impact of Anxious Attachment on Relationships

1. Recognizing Patterns in Relationships:

- Think about your past relationships (romantic, friendships, family). Can you identify any common patterns where your anxious attachment may have influenced the dynamics?

- Write down one specific instance where you felt particularly anxious. What were the circumstances, and how did you respond? Reflect on how recognizing these patterns can help you make healthier choices.

2. Emotional Triggers:

- Reflect on recent interactions where you felt anxious or insecure. What specific actions or words from others triggered these feelings?

- Note three common triggers and consider how these situations make you feel. How do you typically react when these triggers occur? Think about how awareness of these triggers can help you manage your reactions.

3. Impact on Communication:

   - Assess how your anxious attachment style affects your communication with others. Do you tend to over-communicate or seek constant reassurance?
   - Recall a recent conversation where your need for reassurance was evident. How did it impact the interaction, and how did the other person respond? Consider how improving communication can enhance your relationships.

4. Self-Soothing Techniques:

   - Identify techniques or activities that help calm your anxiety in relationships. These might include deep breathing, journaling, or taking a walk.
   - List three self-soothing techniques you can use when feeling anxious. How effective are these methods for you? Reflect on how practicing these techniques can improve your emotional regulation.

5. Seeking Support:

- Consider the role of your support network in managing your anxious attachment. Who are the key people you turn to for support and reassurance?

- Reflect on how these individuals help you navigate your anxiety. Is there a balance between seeking support from others and fostering self-reliance? Think about how strengthening your support network can enhance your resilience.

6. Personal Growth and Learning:

- What steps have you taken to understand and manage your anxious attachment? This might include reading, therapy, or practicing mindfulness.

- List two areas where you feel you have made progress and one where you would like to improve. Reflect on how continuing your personal growth can lead to more secure attachments.

Chapter Three

Communication Strategies for Anxious Attachers

Imagine stepping into a room where everyone speaks a different language, each person trying to convey their thoughts and feelings, yet the words don't seem to align. This scenario, filled with potential misunderstandings and frustrations, is close to what it feels like to navigate communication when you grapple with anxious attachment. The words are there, but the fear of how they'll be received and the anxiety about whether they truly convey what you mean can make every conversation feel like a hurdle. In this chapter, we delve into the art of communication—not just as a means of expressing thoughts but as a bridge to deeper connection, understanding, and relationship harmony. Here, we'll explore how you can articulate your needs confidently and manage the feedback to foster clarity, closeness, and trust.

3.1 Articulating Needs Clearly and Confidently

Develop self-awareness

The journey to effective communication begins with a deep exploration of self-awareness. Understanding your own needs is pivotal, as it sets the foundation for communicating them to others. Reflecting on what triggers your anxiety and what provides comfort can enlighten you about your emotional landscape. Tools like journaling or engaging in mindfulness practices serve as mirrors reflecting your true emotional state, helping you discern the roots of your anxiety. For instance, journaling about times when you felt misunderstood or unsupported can reveal patterns in your emotional responses and needs, guiding you toward understanding what you truly require from your relationships.

Use 'I' statements

Once you understand your needs, the challenge is to communicate them effectively. This is where 'I' statements become a powerful tool. By framing your communication from personal perspective, you avoid placing blame and reduce the potential for defensive reactions. For example, instead of saying, "You don't care about my feelings," consider saying, "I feel hurt when I don't hear from you because it makes me feel uncared for." This method clarifies that you are expressing your feelings about the situation and opens up a space for constructive dialogue instead of conflict.

Practice assertiveness

Assertiveness is about expressing thoughts, feelings, and needs directly, honestly, and respectfully. It's a critical skill, especially for those who tend toward either passivity or aggression when anxious. Consider engaging in role-playing exercises or attending assertiveness training workshops to enhance your assertiveness. These can provide a safe environment to practice stating your needs without overstepping into aggressiveness or retreating into passivity. For example, role-playing a scenario where you must confront a friend about feeling excluded can help you find the right words to express your feelings assertively and respectfully.

Feedback loop

Finally, engaging in a feedback loop is crucial after expressing your needs. It means asking the other person how they perceived your message and being open to their perspective. This process not only clarifies misunderstandings but also deepens mutual understanding. It allows you to adjust your communication if necessary and reinforces the openness in your relationships. For instance, after discussing your need for more frequent check-ins with a partner, ask them how they feel about this request. Their insights can help you understand their capacity and willingness, and together you can find a middle ground that respects both of your needs.

Navigating communication with an anxious attachment style isn't just about making yourself heard. It's about creating pathways that lead to deeper understanding and stronger connections.

As you practice these strategies, you'll find that your communication and relationships begin to reflect more of the security and warmth you seek. Remember, each conversation is a step toward building the confident, connected, and expressive self you aspire to be.

3.2 Listening Skills for Building Deeper Connections

When we think about communication, it's easy to focus mainly on how we express ourselves. However, the art of listening can be even more crucial in nurturing and deepening relationships. It's not just about hearing the words but understanding the complete message, including the emotions and intentions behind it. This deeper level of understanding can transform interactions from simple exchanges of information to meaningful connections that foster trust and intimacy.

Active listening is a skill that requires practice and intentionality. It involves fully concentrating on the speaker, understanding their message, responding thoughtfully, and remembering the information later. One effective technique is maintaining eye contact, which shows the speaker they have your full attention and that you value what they're saying. Nodding along and giving small verbal affirmations like "I see" or "I understand" also reassure the speaker that you are engaged. Another powerful aspect of active listening is paraphrasing—repeating what the speaker has said in your own words. It not only shows that you are listening but also helps you to understand the message accurately. For instance, if a friend tells you about a problem they're facing at work, you might respond, "It sounds like you're feeling really overwhelmed by your workload. What do you think would help lift that pressure?" This response shows that you've processed their feelings and are engaged in finding solutions with them.

Developing empathy is another crucial element of effective listening. Empathy allows you to understand and share another person's feelings, which can significantly deepen your connection. One way to enhance your empathetic responses is to imagine yourself in the speaker's situation. When listening, try to visualize what they are describing and how it might feel to be in their position. This perspective-taking can shift your responses from superficial to genuinely supportive and nurturing. Suppose a partner shares their anxiety about an upcoming job interview. Instead of offering generic advice or reassurance, you might say, "That sounds really stressful. I remember feeling similar when I had my last interview. Would you like to talk through some strategies that helped me?" This kind of empathetic response validates their feelings and offers practical support.

Managing your emotional reactions during conversations is crucial, especially when the topics are sensitive or close to your heart. It's natural to have emotional responses, but unchecked emotions can lead to defensive or aggressive reactions, which can shut down effective communication. To manage this, try to maintain a level of self-awareness during conversations. Recognize when your emotions are intensifying, and if needed, take a moment to breathe and calm yourself before responding. This pause can help you choose responses that contribute to a constructive dialogue rather than escalating tensions.

Listening extends beyond the words spoken. Non-verbal cues—such as facial expressions, posture, and tone of voice—play a significant role in communication. They can often tell you more about how someone feels than their words alone. Paying attention to these cues can help you understand the conveyed message. For example, if someone says they are fine but avoids eye contact and has a closed posture, they might not be as fine as they claim. Recognizing these discrepancies can prompt you to probe gently or offer support, fostering a deeper understanding and connection.

Integrating these listening skills into your interactions enhances your communication abilities and builds stronger, more empathetic relationships. Whether with a friend, family member, or partner, listening deeply and responding with empathetic understanding is invaluable. It transforms everyday interactions into opportunities for connection and growth, paving the way for more fulfilling and supportive relationships.

3.3 Avoiding Misinterpretations and Assumptions

In the intricate dance of communication, it's all too easy for words to spiral into webs of misunderstanding, especially when anxious attachment colors your interactions. Misinterpretations and assumptions can act like invisible rifts that widen with every conversation, potentially leading to feelings of isolation and conflict. To bridge these gaps, fostering a habit of clarity and understanding in your exchanges is vital. Let's explore practical ways to cultivate these habits, ensuring your communications build bridges rather than barriers.

Encouraging the habit of asking clarifying questions is fundamental in dispelling assumptions that often lead to misunderstandings. When in doubt about a partner's comment or a friend's feedback, the instinct might be to fill in the gaps with your own narratives, usually tinted with past insecurities or fears. This is where the cycle of misunderstanding begins. Instead, pose questions that probe deeper into the intent behind the words. For instance, if a partner says something that feels dismissive, instead of spiraling into insecurity, you might ask, "Can you help me understand what you meant when you said that?" This approach clears up immediate doubts and models open communication, showing that you are engaged and seeking proper understanding rather than reacting defensively.

Challenging cognitive distortions such as catastrophizing or overgeneralizing also play a crucial role in clear communication. These mental traps can distort your perception, leading you to expect the worst or to see a pattern based on a single event. Recognizing these distortions in your thought process is the first step. When you catch yourself thinking, "They're late because they don't care," pause and consider more benign possibilities. Perhaps they were simply caught in traffic. To counter these distortions, practice reframing your thoughts to reflect more balanced perspectives. It will alleviate unnecessary anxiety and prevent the buildup of resentment based on unfounded fears.

Taking a step back to consider alternative interpretations is another effective strategy to enrich your understanding and prevent knee-jerk reactions. This perspective-taking can feel counterintuitive, especially when emotions run high. However, allowing yourself to consider different viewpoints creates a space for empathy and reduces the likelihood of misinterpretations. Say a friend cancels your plans at the last minute. Instead of assuming your friendship is unvalued, consider other contexts—perhaps your friend is overwhelmed with personal issues or work stress. This broader view can soften your initial disappointment, paving the way for a supportive rather than accusatory response.

Regular emotional check-ins with those close to you can significantly enhance the clarity and depth of your communications. These check-ins serve as preventive maintenance for your relationships, wherein you can explore feelings and clarify misunderstandings before they escalate. Make it a practice to regularly ask how your friends or partners feel about different aspects of your relationship. This act could be as simple as, "How are we doing? Is there anything on your mind regarding our last conversation that you'd like to clear up?" These conversations can fortify your relationships against the erosive effects of assumptions and provide continual opportunities for growth and understanding.

Integrating these strategies into your daily interactions creates a communicative environment where transparency and empathy prevail over assumptions and fears. Each conversation becomes an opportunity to strengthen your connections, weaving a stronger, more resilient fabric into your relationships.

3.4 The Role of Tone and Body Language in Secure Communication

Our chosen words are just the tip of the iceberg in the nuanced tapestry of human interaction. Beneath the surface, a complex dance of tone, body language, and even the subtlest of touches can convey volumes, often speaking louder than the spoken word. For someone navigating the waters of anxious attachment, learning to understand and consciously manage these non-verbal cues can be transformative, not just in how you communicate but in the very nature of your relationships.

Tone of voice, for example, carries an emotional weight that can dramatically alter the message your words intend to convey. A simple phrase like "I'm here for you" can soothe or sting depending on whether it's spoken with warmth or detachment. For those with anxious attachment who might already be hypersensitive to signs of rejection or disinterest, a seemingly neutral tone can be misread as cold or uncaring. This misinterpretation can trigger a cascade of insecurity and fear, complicating communication. To foster healthier exchanges, listening to the words and how they are said becomes essential. This dual awareness helps accurately gauge the speaker's emotions and intentions, reducing the likelihood of misunderstandings.

Moreover, becoming more mindful of your tone can profoundly impact how your words are received. By consciously infusing your voice with warmth and openness, especially in moments of tension, you can help reassure an anxious partner or friend, reinforcing your support and concern for them. It doesn't mean masking your true feelings but choosing a tone that aligns with your intentions, ensuring your message is heard and felt as intended.

Similarly, body language offers a powerful channel of communication that often bypasses words altogether. A furrowed brow, averted eyes, or crossed arms can signal defensiveness or withdrawal, while an open stance, eye contact, and relaxed posture suggest openness and attentiveness. For someone with an anxious attachment style, reading these signals can sometimes feel like deciphering a complex code, especially when anxiety filters the interpretation through a lens of fear and doubt. Here, the importance of self-monitoring becomes evident. By becoming more aware of your body language and adjusting it to reflect your feelings and intentions more clearly, you can help bridge the emotional gap. For instance, if discussing a sensitive topic, maintaining gentle eye contact and an open posture can convey your engagement and reassure your partner that you are fully present and receptive.

Adjusting your non-verbal communication to convey openness and reassurance involves more than just managing your tone and posture; it extends to the tactile through the use of touch. Touch, when appropriate and consensual, can be a powerful communicator. A gentle hand on the shoulder, a warm hug, or a reassuring squeeze of the hand can communicate support and empathy more profoundly than words. In relationships where anxiety might cloud verbal communication, these small gestures of touch can serve as clear signals of love and support, helping to calm fears and build security.

Navigating the subtle realms of tone, body language, and touch requires a keen awareness and a willingness to adapt. For those managing anxious attachments, this awareness is not just about avoiding misinterpretation; it's about actively building a communication style that supports and enhances your relationships. By aligning your non-verbal cues with your words, you create a harmony in communication that can ease anxiety and foster more profound and secure connections. As you practice these skills, remember that each step forward enriches your interactions and your journey toward more secure and fulfilling relationships.

3.5 Conflict Resolution for Anxious Attachers

Tackling the rocky terrains of conflict can feel particularly daunting if you have an anxious attachment style. The fear of possible outcomes might cloud your judgment, making it challenging to address issues constructively. Preparing for potential conflicts involves more than just bracing yourself for confrontation; it's about understanding your emotional triggers and organizing your thoughts and feelings beforehand. This preparation is not a strategy to win an argument but to ensure the discussion remains respectful and productive. Start by reflecting on past conflicts: what escalated them, what calmed them, and how you felt. Recognize patterns in your reactions and consider more effective responses. For instance, if you notice that being interrupted is a trigger, plan to express calmly at the beginning of the conversation how important it is for you that both parties listen fully before responding.

Focusing on solutions rather than problems during conflicts can significantly shift the dynamics of the discussion. This approach doesn't mean ignoring the issues but emphasizes finding mutual ground and working toward resolutions. When a conflict arises, explicitly ask yourself and the other person, "What outcome are we seeking?" This question can help anchor the conversation and prevent it from veering into less productive territory. For example, if the conflict is about feeling neglected, instead of cataloging every instance of feeling let down, focus on discussing specific ways you can make time for each other moving forward. By directing the conversation toward solutions, you reduce anxiety and build a framework for more constructive interactions.

The timing and setting of a conversation can significantly influence its outcome. Choosing the right moment and environment to discuss sensitive issues can significantly affect how the message is received. Avoid starting potentially heated conversations right as someone walks through the door from work or late at night when both of you are likely tired and less patient. Instead, agree on a time when both of you will likely be calm and have the mental bandwidth to engage in a meaningful discussion. Similarly, ensuring the setting is private and free from interruptions shows respect for the conversation and the relationship. For example, a quiet living room with phones turned off provides a space where both parties can feel safe to express themselves openly.

De-escalation techniques are essential tools to keep conflicts from spiraling. One effective method is taking timeouts—a planned pause in the conversation to allow emotions to settle and perspectives to broaden. If you feel the conversation is getting too heated, suggest a brief break where both parties can take time to breathe and collect their thoughts. During the break, engage in calming activities like deep breathing or a short walk. Also, practice rephrasing statements to be less accusatory. Instead of saying, "You never consider my feelings," try, "I feel upset because I think my feelings weren't considered." This slight modification can prevent the other person from becoming defensive, maintaining a more neutral ground for discussion.

These strategies help manage the immediate challenges of conflict and foster a deeper understanding and respect within relationships. They allow you to express your needs and feelings without letting anxiety dictate the course of the conversation. As you continue to apply these techniques, you'll likely find that your relationships withstand conflicts better and grow stronger and more resilient in the face of challenges.

As we wrap up this exploration of conflict resolution strategies tailored for anxious attachers, remember the overarching goal is not to avoid conflict altogether but to manage it in ways that strengthen your connections. Each conflict can enhance understanding, trust, and intimacy within your relationships. With the tools and insights discussed, you're better equipped to turn potential confrontations into constructive dialogues that nurture rather than strain your connections. The next chapter will build on these communication foundations, exploring deeper emotional connections and how to maintain them to ensure your relationships are as fulfilling and supportive as possible.

Self-Assessment and Reflection Exercise for Chapter 3: Communication Strategies for Anxious Attachers

1. Assessing Your Communication Style:

- Reflect on your typical communication patterns in relationships. How do you usually express your needs and feelings?
  - Identify any recurring issues or conflicts that arise from your communication style. Write down a recent example and consider how recognizing these patterns can help you improve your communication.

2. Recognizing Triggers:

- What specific situations or behaviors from your partner trigger anxious feelings and affect your communication?
  - Describe a recent instance where you felt triggered and how it influenced your communication. Reflect on how understanding these triggers can help you manage your reactions.

3. Evaluating Communication Effectiveness:

- Think about a recent conversation where you felt your needs were not understood. What could you have done differently to express yourself more clearly?
  - Write down three strategies you can use to improve clarity and effectiveness in your communication. Consider how these strategies can enhance your interactions.

4. Practicing Active Listening:

- Recall a recent conversation with your partner. How well did you listen to their perspective without interrupting or planning your response?

- List three techniques you can practice to become a better active listener. Reflect on how improving your listening skills can strengthen your relationships.

5. Developing Assertiveness:

- Reflect on a time when you struggled to communicate your needs assertively. What held you back?
- Identify three ways to practice being more assertive in expressing your needs and boundaries. Consider how assertiveness can lead to healthier relationships.

6. Role-Playing Scenarios:

- Create a hypothetical conversation where you need to communicate an important need or boundary to your partner. Write down both your dialogue and possible responses from your partner.
- Practice this scenario using clear, assertive language and active listening skills. Reflect on how practicing these scenarios can prepare you for real-life conversations.

7. Seeking Feedback:

- Ask a trusted friend or partner for feedback on your communication style. What do they think you do well, and what could you improve?

- Reflect on this feedback and write down one actionable step you will take to enhance your communication. Consider how incorporating feedback can lead to better communication.

Chapter Four

Building Self-Esteem and Personal Identity

Imagine standing before a mirror to glimpse your reflection and look deeper into who you are and what you truly value. This mirror doesn't reflect your physical appearance but the very essence of your inner self. For many of us grappling with anxious attachment, the reflection we see is often clouded by doubts and fears, overshadowing the vibrant person we are meant to be. This chapter is your guide to cleaning that mirror so you can better see and enhance your true self through practices that bolster self-esteem and nurture a positive personal identity. Here we embark on a transformative exploration of self-worth, utilizing tools and exercises to fortify your sense of self and reshape how you interact with the world.

4.1 Exercises for Enhancing Self-Worth

Affirmations and Positive Self-Talk

The journey to greater self-esteem begins with the words you choose to describe your own experience. Words have power—they can lift you up or pull you down. Affirmations and positive self-talk are tools that help you harness this power, steering your thoughts in a more positive direction. An affirmation is a short, powerful statement that, when spoken repeatedly, reinforces the positive aspects of your self-image. For instance, starting your day by affirming, "I am worthy of respect and love," can gradually transform your subconscious beliefs and how you act and react to situations. It's important to cultivate the feeling along with the affirmation. If you struggle at first, think of something with the same feeling tone as your affirmation. Once you have the feeling, repeat your affirmation.

Similarly, positive self-talk involves shifting the narrative from criticism and doubt to support and belief. It's about changing internal dialogues like "I can't do this" to "I am fully capable of handling this challenge." This shift can take a little time and requires consistent practice. It's about catching yourself in the moment of self-doubt and consciously choosing a kinder, more encouraging response. This practice will improve your mood and outlook and significantly impact how you perceive and assert yourself in relationships and other areas of your life.

Engaging fully with your affirmations by infusing them with genuine emotion is essential as it amplifies their impact. When you say affirmations with heartfelt conviction, it strengthens the connection between your words and your subconscious mind and imbues the affirmation with energy that can resonate deeply within you. This emotional engagement makes the affirmation more believable and powerful, accelerating the transformation of your subconscious beliefs. For example, passionately declaring, "I am confident and capable," helps to cement this belief more firmly in your mind, positively influencing your behaviors and attitudes.

Visualization Techniques

Visualization is a potent tool for enhancing self-esteem. It involves creating a vivid mental image of you being in and coming from the visualization, achieving your goals and confidently handling challenging situations. This technique leverages the brain's inability to distinguish between real and imagined events, making it a powerful method for building confidence and rehearsing success. For example, visualize and feel yourself confidently delivering a presentation at work or approaching a new acquaintance easily. See your surroundings as if you were there, or as if you are actually walking towards the new acquaintance. Feel the satisfaction and pride that comes with these achievements. Regular visualization primes your mind to act in ways that align with the positive outcomes you imagine, gradually building your confidence in your capabilities. Engaging your feelings is essential.

Strengths Inventory

Taking inventory of your strengths and accomplishments is like setting up a personal gallery of your successes. This easy exercise involves listing all the strengths, skills, positive qualities, and achievements you are proud of. Reflect on these regularly, especially when doubts and insecurities surface. This practice boosts your morale and provides tangible proof of your capabilities and worth, countering feelings of inadequacy or failure. It's a reminder that you have faced challenges before and emerged stronger, a reassurance that you can handle whatever comes your way.

Role Models and Mentors

Identifying role models or mentors who embody the qualities you admire can significantly influence your path to greater self-esteem. These individuals serve as sources of inspiration and practical guidance, showing you what is possible and how you might navigate your journey. They can be from any sphere of your life—family, friends, professionals, or even historical or public figures. Engage with their stories, learn how they overcame their challenges, and, if possible, seek direct mentorship. This connection motivates you and provides a framework for developing and embodying similar qualities, reinforcing your belief in your potential and worth.

Incorporating these exercises into your daily routine can transform how you view yourself and interact with the world. They empower you to rewrite the narrative of your life, turning self-doubt into self-assurance, fear into courage, and insecurity into a well-founded confidence that enhances every aspect of your life. As you practice these techniques, remember that each step forward, no matter how small, is a leap toward the person you are capable of becoming—a person who views themselves with clarity, accepts themselves with compassion, and presents themselves with unshakeable confidence.

4.2 Setting and Achieving Personal Goals

When you set out to achieve your dreams, the path can often seem daunting, like standing at the base of a towering mountain. It's not just the vision of reaching the peak that will propel you forward but also your strategy for the climb. The SMART goals framework offers a structured approach to breaking down your aspirations into achievable milestones. SMART stands for Specific, Measurable, Achievable, Relevant, and Time-bound. Each component is crucial in clarifying your objectives and setting a realistic path to reach them. For instance, instead of setting a vague goal like "I want to be more fit," a SMART goal would be "I'll jog for 30 minutes three times a week for the next two months." This goal is specific (jogging), measurable (30 minutes, three times a week), achievable (a realistic increase in activity), relevant (contributes to overall health), and time-bound (two months). By framing your goals within these parameters, you set clear expectations and enhance your ability to track progress and adjust as needed.

Breaking down larger goals into smaller, manageable tasks will help keep you from becoming overwhelmed while maintaining your motivation. Think of it as creating a roadmap where each small task is another step toward your ultimate destination. For example, if your goal is to write a book, start by setting weekly targets for writing a chapter outline, then proceed to detailed character sketches, and so on. Each completed task brings a sense of achievement and keeps the larger project from becoming too daunting. This method keeps your journey organized and sprinkles it with regular doses of accomplishment, fueling your drive forward.

Accountability is another cornerstone of successful goal setting. Sharing your goals with a supportive friend, family member, or group can significantly increase your chances of success. They can provide encouragement, offer advice, and help keep you on track. Moreover, consider maintaining a goal journal where you regularly document your progress and reflect on the challenges and successes. This record keeps you accountable and serves as a motivational archive, reminding you of how far you've come whenever discouragement looms.

Celebrating progress, regardless of the size of the achievement, is vital in sustaining your momentum. Each milestone you reach is a testament to your commitment and effort. Acknowledge these moments with a reward, whether a small treat, a day off, or sharing your success with friends and family. These celebrations reinforce positive emotions associated with accomplishment and can boost your self-esteem, making the journey as rewarding as the destination. Integrating these practices into your life empowers you to dream big and turn those dreams into reality.

4.3 The Importance of Self-Care in Building Self-Esteem

Self-care is more than a buzzword. It's a vital practice that supports your mental health and bolsters your self-esteem, providing a foundation for success in all areas of your life. At its core, self-care involves activities and practices you engage in deliberately to take care of your mental, emotional, and physical health. It's important to distinguish genuine self-care from mere self-indulgence. Self-indulgence often involves activities that provide immediate gratification but do not necessarily support your overall well-being, like excessive shopping or overeating. Genuine self-care, on the other hand, nourishes and rejuvenates your body and mind and aligns with your long-term values and needs.

Incorporating varied self-care activities into your routine can cater to different aspects of your well-being. For your physical health, regular exercise like yoga, jogging, or even simple stretches can increase your physical vitality and enhance your mood by releasing endorphins. To support your mental health, practices such as meditation, reading, or engaging in hobbies that challenge and fulfill you can be tremendously beneficial. Emotional self-care might include keeping a gratitude journal, practicing mindfulness, or scheduling regular check-ins with a therapist. These activities help manage stress, allow you to process emotions more effectively, and foster a balanced lifestyle.

The link between regular self-care practices and self-respect is profound. Engaging in self-care is a declaration that you value yourself and deserve the time and effort these practices require. This practice can be particularly empowering if you struggle with self-esteem because it reinforces your worth and autonomy. Consistently caring for yourself teaches you that your needs matter and that you are capable of meeting them. Over time, this builds a robust sense of self-worth that permeates all areas of your life, enhancing how you interact with others and handle challenges.

However, dedicating time to self-care can sometimes stir up guilt, especially if you perceive it as a luxury rather than a necessity. This guilt can be even more pronounced if you have responsibilities such as work or caring for a family that demands much of your time. Overcoming this guilt involves shifting your perspective to view self-care as essential to your well-being. Recognize that by caring for yourself, you are improving your health and happiness and enhancing your capacity to care for others. Strategies to overcome self-care guilt include:

- Setting specific and manageable goals for self-care.
- Communicating your self-care needs to others.
- Gradually integrate these practices into your routine to demonstrate their positive impacts on your life.

Remember, self-care is not selfish; it is an essential practice that enables you to be your best self for yourself and those around you. It really is crucial to recharge and take care of your needs first. If you are empty, then what exactly can you give to another?

4.4 Overcoming the Fear of Rejection

Rejection is a word that often sends a shiver down the spine, bringing with it a flood of insecurity and doubt. For those with an anxious attachment style, the fear of rejection can be particularly paralyzing, influencing not only how you view relationships but also how you perceive yourself. Understanding the origins of this fear is crucial. It often stems from early experiences when acceptance was equated with love and approval and rejection with a loss of these vital connections. This formative conditioning instills a deep-seated fear that rejection in any context might mean you are inherently unlovable or inadequate.

This fear does not have to dictate your life. One practical approach to diminish the power of fear is through exposure therapy, a technique often used to treat various anxiety disorders. The premise is simple yet powerful: by gradually and repeatedly exposing yourself to small, controlled experiences of rejection, you can desensitize your emotional response to it. Start small—perhaps by asking a friend a favor they might refuse or making a request in a public setting that somebody could decline. These controlled exposures can significantly reduce the anxiety associated with rejection, as repeated experiences often demonstrate that the aftermath of rejection is rarely as catastrophic as we fear. More importantly, these situations provide a real-time opportunity to practice handling and processing rejection in healthy and constructive ways.

Another transformative strategy is reframing how you view rejection. Typically, rejection is seen as a direct reflection of our worth, but this perspective is limiting and distorted. Instead, try to view rejection as a normal part of life—an experience that does not define your worth but shapes your path. Cognitive-behavioral techniques can be particularly effective in this reframing process. For instance, when faced with rejection, instead of defaulting to self-criticism, challenge yourself to find neutral or positive explanations for the rejection. Perhaps the rejection was less about you and more about the other person's preferences, circumstances, or needs. This shift in perspective can mitigate the pain associated with rejection and foster a more resilient self-view.

Viewing rejection as an opportunity for growth is one of the most constructive ways to handle this fear. Each rejection offers valuable insights into your desires, strengths, and areas for improvement. For example, if rejected after a job interview, instead of ruminating on your perceived inadequacies, analyze the experience to identify areas for professional growth or aspects of the interview that you could improve next time. This approach lessens the sting of rejection and empowers you to use the experience as a stepping stone for personal and professional development. This kind of constructive self-reflection can transform potentially negative experiences into powerful catalysts for self-enhancement and confidence building.

By embracing these strategies, you begin to loosen the grip that fear of rejection has on your life. Each step forward in understanding, confronting, and reframing rejection enriches your self-esteem and fortifies your resilience, enabling you to navigate life's challenges with greater confidence and less fear. As you continue to grow and learn through these experiences, you gradually transform the once daunting experience of rejection into a manageable, even beneficial aspect of your journey toward self-discovery and personal empowerment.

4.5 Celebrating Self-Achievements and Milestones

Recognizing and celebrating your achievements, no matter how minor they seem, is essential in building and maintaining your self-esteem. Each accomplishment, big or small, is a building block in the foundation of your self-worth and a stepping stone toward more significant successes. When you take the time to acknowledge your accomplishments, you reinforce to yourself that you are capable, that your efforts matter, and that progress, in any form, is worthy of celebration. This act of recognition not only boosts your mood but also propels you forward on your path of personal growth.

Creating personal rituals for celebrating achievements can significantly enhance the emotional impact of these milestones. Rituals can make the celebration a more tangible and impactful experience, deeply embedding these positive moments into your memory. For instance, you might decide to write a celebratory note to yourself for each achievement, detailing what you did and why it matters and keeping it in a "success" jar. Alternatively, you might create a ritual to treat yourself to a favorite activity or item as a reward for reaching a milestone. The key is consistency and personal significance—choose rituals that are meaningful to you, excite you, and make striving toward your goals as rewarding as reaching them.

Sharing your successes with friends, family, or a supportive community serves multiple purposes. It not only allows you to externalize and reinforce your achievements but also helps to strengthen your social bonds. Sharing your triumphs can inspire others and invite them to celebrate with you, multiplying the joy. Moreover, it encourages a supportive environment where others feel comfortable sharing and celebrating their successes, fostering a community of mutual encouragement. Whether it's a small win like sticking to your workout routine or a significant one like receiving a promotion, sharing these moments can amplify your positive emotions and deepen your connections with those around you.

Reflective journaling is a powerful tool to record and reflect on your achievements over time. This practice involves regularly documenting your successes and your steps to achieve them. Over time, this journal becomes a personal ledger of growth, a concrete record of your progress. Reviewing this journal can be incredibly uplifting, especially during moments of doubt or when facing new challenges. It reminds you of your capabilities and resilience, boosting your confidence and motivating you to continue pushing forward. Moreover, this form of journaling encourages continuous self-reflection, helping you understand what strategies work best for you and how to apply them to future goals.

In celebrating your achievements, you build stronger self-esteem and create a positive feedback loop that propels you toward future success. Each celebration reinforces your belief in your abilities and motivates you to pursue further goals, continuing your personal development and self-discovery path. As you move forward, let each achievement, no matter the size, be a cause for celebration, a moment to pause and remind yourself of your worth and capabilities.

As this chapter closes, remember the importance of recognizing every step forward and honoring your journey and efforts. These celebrations are not just about marking achievements; they affirm your growth, resilience, and potential. As you transition into the next chapter, carry with you the understanding that each achievement is a testament to your ability to shape and direct your own life, reflect on your evolving relationship with yourself, and be a beacon guiding you toward even greater success.

Self-Assessment and Reflection Exercises for Chapter 4: Building Self-Esteem and Personal Identity

1. Identifying Strengths and Accomplishments:

- Activity: List five strengths and five accomplishments that make you proud. Briefly explain why each strength or accomplishment is important to you.

- This exercise helps you focus on your positive qualities and achievements, reinforcing your self-worth and highlighting your capabilities.

2. Daily Affirmations:

- Activity: Create three positive affirmations that resonate with you. Repeat these affirmations every morning for a week and journal any changes you notice in your mood or self-perception.

- Affirmations help reprogram negative thinking patterns and promote a positive self-image, fostering greater self-esteem over time.

3. Visualization Practice:

- Activity: Spend a few minutes each day visualizing a scenario where you feel confident and successful. Please write down the details of this visualization and how it makes you feel.
- Visualization reinforces positive imagery in your mind, helping you to embody confidence and success in real-life situations.

4. Tracking Positive Experiences:

Activity: Keep a daily journal in which you note one positive experience or something you did well each day. Reflect on how these experiences make you feel about yourself.
- This practice helps shift your focus toward positive experiences, building a habit of recognizing and appreciating your strengths and contributions.

5. Exploring Role Models:

- Activity: Identify one role model or mentor who embodies qualities you admire. Write about what you can learn from their example and how you can incorporate these qualities into your own life.

- Learning from role models can inspire you to develop similar qualities and provide a roadmap for personal growth, enhancing your self-esteem and personal identity.

Completing these exercises will help you gain deeper insights into your strengths and accomplishments, cultivate positive thinking, and draw inspiration from role models. This self-assessment will also help you build a stronger sense of self-worth and identity.

Chapter Five

Practical Exercises for Managing Anxiety in Attachments

Have you ever paused to consider how the simple act of writing down your thoughts could transform your emotional landscape, particularly in how you connect and interact with others? Imagine holding a pen poised over a blank page, the tip just touching the paper—a threshold moment where introspection meets expression. Journaling for emotional processing is a practice that can provide profound insight into the anxious attachment style and help smooth the edges of your relational experiences. In this chapter, we delve into the therapeutic art of journaling, guiding you through structured approaches and reflective techniques designed to enhance your understanding of yourself and improve your relationships.

5.1 Daily Journaling Prompts for Emotional Processing

Introduction to Therapeutic Journaling

Journaling is more than just a record of events; it's a tool for deep emotional processing. Translating your thoughts and feelings into words engages different parts of your brain, helping you see your experiences from new perspectives and understand them more clearly. This practice can be particularly beneficial if you're dealing with anxious attachment, as it allows you to explore and clarify your emotions, recognize patterns in your thoughts and behaviors, and reflect on your interactions with others. Writing slows down your thought processes, giving you the time to examine your feelings without judgment. It can lead to significant revelations about why you react the way you do in relationships and help you develop strategies for managing your anxiety.

Structured Prompts

To harness the full potential of journaling, specific prompts designed to explore your attachment-related fears and patterns can be particularly effective. Consider starting with prompts that encourage you to delve into your emotional responses to daily interactions. For example:

"Today I felt anxious about my relationship when..."

"The thought that often makes me feel insecure is..."

"A situation that triggered my anxiety today involved…"

"When I feel anxious, my typical response is to…"

These prompts can help you trace the roots of your anxiety, helping you recognize specific triggers and situations in which your anxious attachment style is most pronounced. Regularly responding to these prompts creates a valuable repository of insights about your emotional triggers and the contexts in which they arise.

Guidance on Consistency

The benefits of journaling are compounded when practiced consistently. Making journaling a daily habit helps you track your emotional fluctuations and patterns over time, providing a clearer picture of your progress in managing attachment anxiety. To integrate journaling into your daily routine, set a specific time each day for this practice, perhaps in the morning to set a reflective tone for the day or in the evening as a way to decompress. Keep your journal where you'll see it often and consider setting a reminder on your phone. It's also helpful to create a comfortable and inviting space for journaling—a quiet corner with a cozy chair, a pleasant notebook, and a pen that feels good in your hand can make the practice something you look forward to each day.

Reflective Analysis

Analyzing the entries in your journal can transform what might feel like random thoughts into actionable insights. Set aside time each week to review your writing, looking for recurring themes or patterns. Ask yourself:

"What emotions come up most frequently in my entries?"

"Are there specific relationships or situations that trigger my anxiety?"

"How have I responded to moments of anxiety and what were the outcomes?"

"What new understandings have I gained about my attachment style?"

This reflective analysis is crucial as it helps you track your emotional growth, understand your triggers more deeply, and recognize how your responses to anxiety have evolved. Over time, this practice can lead to greater self-awareness and more effective management of your attachment-related anxieties.

As you continue to explore and apply these journaling strategies, remember that each entry is a step forward on your path to emotional clarity and relationship fulfillment. Through the simple act of writing, you are taking control of your narrative, reshaping your attachment experiences, and opening up new possibilities for connection and growth.

5.2 Mindfulness Practices for Relationship Anxiety

Navigating the often choppy waters of relationships can feel daunting, especially when undercurrents of anxiety threaten to unsettle the harmony you strive to maintain. Mindfulness, a practice with roots in ancient traditions and refined by modern psychology, offers a beacon of calm, guiding you to a state of awareness and balance that can transform your relational dynamics. At its core, mindfulness is cultivating a presence fully attuned to the here and now, observing your thoughts and feelings without judgment. This practice can be particularly transformative for managing relationship anxiety, as it encourages you to respond to situations with clarity and insight rather than being swept away by emotional turbulence.

One of the foundational techniques of mindfulness is focused breathing, which can serve as an anchor, steadying your mind amidst the swirl of anxious thoughts. A simple yet effective exercise you can try involves deep, diaphragmatic breathing. Sit comfortably or lie down, place one hand on your stomach and the other on your chest, and take a slow, deep breath in through your nose, feeling your stomach rise more than your chest. Hold this breath for a moment, then exhale slowly through your mouth, feeling your belly lower. Repeat this pattern for a few minutes, focusing solely on the movement of your breath. This breathing technique can help reduce immediate symptoms of anxiety by activating your body's natural relaxation response, providing a sense of calm that can help you approach your relationships from a place of stability rather than insecurity.

Incorporating mindfulness into your conversations can also significantly enhance how you connect with others, especially if anxiety often colors your interactions. Mindful listening involves:

- Fully focusing on the other person.

- Paying attention not only to their words but also to their tone of voice.

- Observing facial expressions and body language.

Mindfulness requires you to be fully present, temporarily setting aside your reactions and judgments to hear what the other person is truly saying. Practicing this kind of listening can help you understand your partner or friend more deeply and respond more appropriately to their needs and emotions, reducing misunderstandings and conflicts that anxiety might otherwise escalate.

Another powerful mindfulness technique is the 'Body Scan' meditation, which can heighten your awareness of the physical sensations accompanying emotional states, including anxiety. To practice a body scan, find a quiet place to lie down or sit comfortably. Close your eyes and focus slowly on each part of your body, starting from your toes and moving upward to the crown of your head. Notice any sensations you feel, such as tension, warmth, or discomfort, without trying to change them. This practice can be particularly insightful for identifying how anxiety manifests in your body, allowing you to address these physical sensations directly through relaxation techniques or further mindfulness practice.

By integrating these mindfulness practices into your daily routine, you can develop a greater awareness of your moment-to-moment experiences internally and your interactions with others. This heightened awareness can empower you to manage relationship anxiety more effectively, fostering a sense of peace that enhances your connections with others and yourself. As you continue to explore these practices, you may find that what once felt overwhelming is now becoming manageable, and your relationships are flourishing in an atmosphere of mutual understanding and respect.

5.3 Role-Playing Scenarios for Secure Attachment Behaviors

Role-playing, a method often used in therapeutic settings, extends beyond its traditional confines to offer significant benefits for individuals seeking to enhance their relationship dynamics. This technique allows you to rehearse responses in various situations, providing a safe space to explore and modify behaviors linked to anxious attachment. Imagine role-playing as a rehearsal for real-life interactions, where you can experiment with different ways of responding to situations that typically trigger your anxiety. This controlled environment is invaluable as it allows you to practice without the immediate real-world consequences, helping you build confidence in your ability to handle similar situations in your daily life.

Developing realistic scenarios for role-playing begins with identifying situations that commonly trigger your anxious attachment responses. These might include scenarios where you feel rejected, typically leading to misunderstandings or moments where you feel overly dependent on a partner's reassurance. For instance, you might create a scenario where you must respond to a partner who has canceled plans, which has triggered a fear of abandonment in the past. You can prepare yourself to handle these situations more effectively by scripting them out. It's about crafting responses that promote open communication, assert your needs, and foster mutual understanding while maintaining emotional balance.

The involvement of a trusted friend or partner in these role-playing exercises can significantly enhance their effectiveness. This collaboration allows for real-time feedback and support, helping you refine your approach to difficult conversations. Choose a partner who understands your goals and is willing to engage in the process thoughtfully. As you role-play, encourage your partner to provide honest feedback to your responses, highlighting both the strengths and the areas where you might still reflect anxious tendencies. This feedback is crucial as it allows for an outside perspective on your behaviors, offering insights you might overlook.

Self-evaluation is an important component of role-playing exercises. After each session, take the time to reflect on your performance. Ask yourself, "How did I handle my emotions during the interaction?" "Did I communicate my needs clearly?" "How did I react to feedback?" This self-reflection enables you to identify which responses were effective and which ones you could improve. Adjustments include refining your tone, being more assertive, or finding more constructive ways to express your feelings. This continual process of evaluation and adjustment fosters a learning mindset, which is crucial for anyone working toward developing secure attachment behaviors.

Through role-playing, you practice new behaviors and begin to internalize them, making it easier to transfer these behaviors into your everyday interactions. This practice can be transformative, turning previously anxiety-inducing interactions into opportunities to strengthen your relationships and build confidence in your ability to maintain emotional equilibrium. As you integrate these role-playing strategies into your repertoire, your relationships will become more stable and fulfilling, marked by an increased ability to handle the complexities of emotional attachment with grace and resilience.

5.4 Using Cognitive Behavioral Techniques to Challenge Anxious Thoughts

Cognitive Behavioral Therapy (CBT) is a form of psychological treatment that has proven highly effective in managing anxiety, especially when it stems from troubled relationship dynamics. At its core, CBT focuses on the interplay between your thoughts, emotions, and behaviors, teaching you to dismantle the negative patterns that have kept you trapped in cycles of anxiety. This approach is grounded in the idea that our thoughts significantly influence how we feel and behave and that we can change our emotional responses and actions by changing our thought patterns. For those grappling with anxious attachment, understanding and applying CBT principles can provide a powerful toolkit for transforming relationship anxiety into healthier, more secure attachment experiences.

One of the first steps in harnessing the power of CBT is to identify the cognitive distortions that fuel your attachment anxiety. Cognitive distortions are irrational thought patterns that often skew your perception of reality, typically in a way that makes situations seem worse than they are. Common distortions include 'mind reading,' where you assume you know what others are thinking without sufficient evidence, and 'catastrophizing,' where you predict the worst possible outcome. For example, if a partner delays responding to a text, you might instantly think, "They're ignoring me because they don't care," a classic case of mind reading combined with catastrophizing. By labeling these thoughts as distortions, you can begin to question their validity and reduce their impact on your emotions and behaviors.

Challenging these unhelpful thoughts is the next crucial step in CBT. This process, known as 'cognitive restructuring,' involves examining your anxious thoughts, assessing their accuracy, and replacing them with more balanced and rational thoughts. Start by writing down specific anxious thoughts that frequently arise in your relationships. Ask yourself: "What evidence do I have that supports this thought? Is there evidence that contradicts it? What would I tell a friend if they had this thought?" This kind of questioning can help you see that your initial thoughts are often based more on fear than fact. For instance, instead of sticking with the thought, "They're ignoring me," you might reframe it to, "They might be busy right now, but I know they care about me because they regularly show affection and make time for me."

Behavioral experiments are another effective technique used in CBT, allowing you to test the validity of your beliefs about attachments and relationships. These experiments involve putting your revised thoughts into action and observing the outcomes. For example, suppose you often feel that expressing your needs will drive people away. In that case, you might experiment by communicating a small need or concern to a friend or partner in a straightforward and respectful manner. The outcome will provide real-life evidence that challenges or supports your belief, helping further reshape your thinking patterns. Most find that their fears of negative outcomes are exaggerated, and these experiments provide concrete proof that not only can they express their needs safely, but doing so often strengthens rather than harms their relationships.

As you continue to apply these CBT strategies, you'll likely notice a gradual decrease in your relationship anxiety and an improvement in your interactions. The key is consistency and honesty in applying these techniques, even when it feels challenging. Over time, the combination of understanding cognitive distortions, practicing thought challenging, and conducting behavioral experiments can significantly alter the landscape of your relationships, turning anxiety and uncertainty into opportunities for growth and deeper connection. This transformative process is not just about managing moments of anxiety but about building a foundation of thought patterns that support healthy, secure attachments.

5.5 Creating a Personalized Anxiety Management Plan

The nuanced journey of managing your anxiety, particularly when it stems from anxious attachment, calls for a personalized approach. Every individual experiences and reacts to anxiety in uniquely personal ways, which means that a one-size-fits-all solution is less likely to be effective. Creating a plan that acknowledges your specific triggers and habitual responses allows you to address the root causes of your anxiety more directly and effectively. This tailored plan isn't just about coping with moments of stress; it's about building a lifestyle that supports ongoing emotional stability and healthier relational dynamics.

To begin crafting your personalized anxiety management plan, start by identifying your unique triggers. These could be specific situations, interactions, or even times of the day when your anxiety tends to spike. Reflect on recent episodes of anxiety and try to pinpoint what preceded these feelings. Was it a text message left unanswered, an offhand comment made by a colleague, or perhaps a date that didn't go as planned? Recognizing these triggers is the first step in developing strategies to manage them. For instance, if unanswered texts are a trigger, part of your plan might include setting rational expectations for communication in your relationships and discussing these with your partner or friends.

Integrating daily techniques that reinforce your new skills is crucial for the efficacy of your management plan. Techniques such as mindfulness can help you maintain calm awareness throughout the day, making you less likely to react impulsively to triggers. Journaling can provide ongoing insights into your emotional patterns and progress. Incorporating regular cognitive-behavioral exercises can help you continually challenge and refine your thought processes, reducing the likelihood of falling back into old, anxiety-driven patterns. Making these practices part of your daily routine ensures that your anxiety management is consistent and rooted in your everyday life, enhancing its effectiveness and sustainability.

Setting long-term goals is essential for maintaining motivation and tracking your progress. These goals should be specific, measurable, achievable, relevant, and time-bound (SMART). Perhaps you aim to reduce the frequency of anxiety attacks, improve your ability to communicate needs without fear or develop healthier responses to triggers. Whatever your goals, outline them clearly in your plan and set periodic milestones to assess your progress. This will keep you focused and allow you to adjust your strategies as needed, ensuring that your approach evolves along with your emotional and relational needs.

The support systems you engage with will play a significant role in your anxiety management. While self-help techniques are powerful, the support of friends, family, or professionals can provide additional perspectives and encouragement. Identify individuals who understand your challenges and are committed to supporting you. These may include a therapist specializing in anxiety disorders or attachment issues, supportive friends who respect your journey, or support groups where you can connect with others facing similar challenges. Engaging with these support systems can provide valuable feedback, prevent feelings of isolation, and reinforce your commitment to your management plan.

As you progress with your personalized anxiety management plan, remember that the ultimate goal is to cultivate a life in which you feel secure, valued, and emotionally balanced. This chapter is designed to give you the tools and insights necessary to craft a plan that addresses your immediate anxiety and supports your long-term emotional health and relationship success. As we close this chapter and prepare to explore the dynamics of attachment and personal growth, carry with you the understanding that managing anxiety is not just about alleviating symptoms but about enriching your entire approach to life and relationships.

Self-Assessment and Reflection Exercises for Chapter 5: Practical Exercises for Managing Anxiety in Attachments

1. Daily Journaling Prompts for Emotional Processing

   - Exercise: For one week, respond to the following daily journaling prompts:

     - "Today I felt anxious about my relationship when…"
     - "The thought that often makes me feel insecure is…"
     - "A situation that triggered my anxiety today involved…"
     - "When I feel anxious, my typical response is to…"

   - Reflection: At the end of the week, review your entries. Identify any recurring themes or patterns in your triggers and responses.

   - Purpose: This exercise helps you trace the roots of your anxiety, recognize specific triggers, and develop awareness of your habitual responses.

2. Mindfulness Meditation Practice

  - Exercise: Dedicate 10 minutes each day to a mindfulness meditation practice. Focus on your breath, and gently bring your attention back whenever your mind wanders.

   - Reflection: After each session, write a brief note about how you felt before and after the meditation. Did it help in reducing your anxiety?

   - Purpose: Mindfulness meditation can help in grounding yourself, reducing anxiety, and increasing emotional regulation.

3. Strengths and Achievements Journal

- Exercise: Create a journal dedicated to your strengths and achievements. Each day, write down at least one personal strength or something you accomplished that day.
- Reflection: Review your entries weekly and consider how recognizing your strengths and achievements affects your anxiety levels.
- Purpose: This exercise boosts self-esteem and provides tangible proof of your capabilities, countering feelings of inadequacy.

4. Role-Playing Scenarios

- Exercise: With a trusted friend or partner, role-play scenarios that typically trigger your anxiety. Practice responding in ways that promote secure attachment behaviors.
- Reflection: After each role-playing session, discuss with your partner how you felt during the exercise and what you learned.
- Purpose: Role-playing helps you rehearse and internalize healthier responses to anxiety-inducing situations.

5. Creating a Personalized Anxiety Management Plan

- Exercise: Develop a personalized plan that includes your specific triggers, coping strategies, and support systems. Include steps to take when you feel anxious and how to seek help if needed.

- Reflection: Revisit and adjust your plan weekly based on your experiences and its effectiveness.

- Purpose: Having a structured plan helps in proactively managing anxiety and provides a clear course of action during stressful times.

6. Visualization of Success

- Exercise: Spend a few minutes each day visualizing yourself successfully handling an anxiety-inducing situation. Focus on the details of how you feel, what you say, and how you act.

- Reflection: Note any changes in your confidence and anxiety levels over time.

- Purpose: Visualization can build confidence and reinforce positive outcomes, making real-life situations feel more manageable.

7. Support System Mapping

Exercise: Draw a map of your current support system. Include friends, family, therapists, and any groups you belong to. Identify gaps where additional support might be beneficial.

- Reflection: Plan how to fill these gaps and strengthen your support network.

- Purpose: Understanding and improving your support system ensures you have the necessary resources during times of anxiety.

By incorporating these exercises into your routine, you can gain deeper insights into your anxiety patterns, develop practical strategies for managing anxiety, and build a robust support system to aid your journey toward secure attachment.

Would you take a moment to give my book an honest review?

Dear Reader,

As you know, Amazon's algorithm thrives on them. By leaving a review for this book, you'll be helping others discover it, which can help them feel the best they deserve to feel, too. Your review will make a significant difference for everyone.

It's very straightforward. Just click on this link to go straight to the review page: https://mybook.to/BmkN

Or scan the QR code with your phone if easier.

Thank you for your support!

Chapter Six

Healing from Past Relationship Trauma

Imagine standing at the edge of a calm lake, its surface a perfect mirror reflecting the sky above. Now imagine throwing a stone into that lake—the ripples distort the reflection, making it hard to see clearly. Our past traumas are like those stones, and our current emotional state, the ripples they create. To see ourselves and our relationships clearly, we must address the disturbances created by these past experiences. This chapter is devoted to helping you identify and understand the triggers linked to past traumas, empowering you to smooth out the waters and restore calm to your emotional landscape.

6.1 Identifying Triggers in Your Relationship Patterns

Mapping Personal History

Consider your relationship history as a map with landmarks representing significant emotional experiences. Some landmarks are bright and joyful, while past hurts might shadow others. By mapping these experiences you can identify patterns that may signal unresolved traumas influencing your current behaviors and relationships. List significant romantic and platonic relationships and note any repetitive outcomes or feelings. For instance, you might find a pattern of feeling abandoned or a tendency to withdraw emotionally when getting close to someone. These patterns are clues pointing toward underlying issues that need your attention.

Recognizing Emotional Triggers

As you reflect on these patterns, try to pinpoint specific situations, behaviors, or emotional responses that consistently trigger discomfort or anxiety. These triggers are often tied to past traumas and can manifest as intense emotional reactions to seemingly benign interactions. For example, you might feel an overwhelming fear of rejection when someone doesn't immediately return a call, stemming from an experience where you felt abandoned. Recognizing these triggers is the first step in disentangling your present emotions from past pains, allowing you to respond to current situations based on reality, not past fears.

Journaling for Trigger Tracking

Maintaining a detailed journal will help deepen your understanding of these triggers. Document instances when your triggers are activated, noting the context of your feelings and your reactions. This practice can help you identify what triggers you, how you react, and what thoughts or beliefs drive those reactions. For instance, if a canceled date leads to anxiety, write about what fears this cancellation stirs in you—are you thinking, "This always happens to me," or perhaps, "They must not care about me"? Over time, this journal will become a valuable tool for recognizing and modifying your automatic reactions to triggers.

Professional Assessments

While self-exploration through journaling and reflection is invaluable, some traumas and their triggers can be deeply buried, not easily accessible through introspection alone. In such cases, seeking a professional psychological assessment can be highly beneficial. Using tools and techniques designed to probe deeper into your subconscious, psychologists and therapists can help uncover layers of emotional injury that might be invisible to you. These assessments can provide insights into your triggers, personality, and coping mechanisms, offering a comprehensive understanding essential for healing.

Engaging with these processes requires courage and commitment, but the rewards—greater self-awareness, improved relationships, and a more stable emotional life—are profound. As you continue to explore these dimensions, remember that each step forward, no matter how small, is a step toward reclaiming your emotional equilibrium and forging a path to healthier, more fulfilling relationships.

6.2 Therapeutic Techniques for Addressing Past Traumas

Navigating the intricate process of healing from past traumas requires more than time—it necessitates targeted therapeutic interventions that address both the psychological and physiological facets of trauma. Specific modalities are effective in treating attachment-related traumas among the myriad of therapeutic approaches. Eye Movement Desensitization and Reprocessing (EMDR), psychodynamic therapy, and cognitive behavioral therapy (CBT) are noteworthy for their proven benefits.

EMDR is a powerful and unique therapeutic approach that has acquired widespread acclaim for its ability to alleviate the distress associated with traumatic memories. It involves the guided recall of trauma-related imagery while simultaneously focusing on an external stimulus, typically side-to-side eye movements, hand-tapping, or auditory tones. This process facilitates the brain's natural adaptive information processing abilities, helping you to reframe the emotional impact of past experiences. The effectiveness of EMDR lies in its potential to change the emotional response to memories of past traumas, making it a powerful tool for those whose attachment issues are rooted in early life distress.

Psychodynamic therapy delves deep into exploring how your early childhood experiences influence your current self. This form of therapy focuses on uncovering the roots of emotional suffering and is particularly suited to addressing attachment traumas that stem from your relationships with primary caregivers. Through the therapeutic relationship, you can explore unresolved conflicts, dysfunctional patterns, and the unconscious dynamics that underpin your attachments. This insight-oriented approach helps you understand and resolve these issues, providing a foundation for healthier future relationships.

Cognitive behavioral therapy (CBT), on the other hand, offers a more structured approach. It focuses on identifying and challenging the negative thoughts and behaviors that arise from and perpetuate your attachment issues. CBT helps you develop healthier cognitive responses through strategies like cognitive restructuring and behavioral experiments, which are particularly effective in tackling the self-defeating thoughts and behaviors typical of anxious attachment styles.

Complementing Therapy with Self-Help Strategies

While these therapies provide robust frameworks for healing, integrating self-help strategies into your daily life can enhance your recovery and empower you to manage symptoms independently. Mindfulness-based stress reduction (MBSR) is one such strategy that has proven effective in reducing anxiety and improving emotional regulation. By cultivating an acute awareness of the present moment, mindfulness helps you disengage from harmful patterns of rumination and worry associated with past traumas. Regular mindfulness practice can significantly diminish the intensity of emotional reactions to triggers, providing a sense of calm and stability.

Self-compassion exercises also play a crucial role in the healing process. Developing compassion toward yourself can be transformative, especially if you tend to be self-critical or blame yourself for past relationship failures. Techniques such as writing letters to yourself from a compassionate perspective or practicing guided meditations focusing on self-kindness can help rebuild your self-esteem and foster a gentle acceptance of your past experiences.

The Role of a Therapist in Your Healing Process

While self-help strategies are invaluable, the guidance of a qualified therapist is irreplaceable, especially when dealing with complex traumas. A therapist provides a safe space to explore painful memories and brings professional insight to help you navigate the maze of your emotions. Choosing the right therapist is paramount—look for someone who specializes in attachment issues and trauma and with whom you feel a strong sense of trust and comfort. It's also beneficial to seek a therapist trained in the specific modalities that resonate with you, whether EMDR, psychodynamic therapy, or CBT.

Integrative Healing Approaches

Consider integrative approaches that combine talk therapy with body-centered therapies for a holistic recovery. Somatic experiencing, for example, is a therapeutic approach that emphasizes the body's role in trauma recovery. It helps you develop awareness of bodily sensations and release tension and trauma stored in the body through gentle exercises and movements. Integrating such body-centered therapies with traditional talk therapies can address the physiological aspects of trauma, aiding in a more comprehensive healing process.

By engaging with these therapeutic techniques and complementing them with self-help strategies, you lay down a path for a thorough and sustainable healing process. This approach addresses the symptoms of your past traumas and fosters a deeper understanding of your emotional patterns, ultimately leading you toward a future where your relationships are no longer shadows of your past but reflections of your true self.

6.3 The Role of Forgiveness in Healing

Forgiveness is often misunderstood as a sign of weakness or an excuse for others' harmful actions. However, forgiveness is a potent tool in personal trauma and recovery that serves a deeper purpose. It is not about condoning unacceptable behavior or denying the pain caused; instead, it is about releasing the burden of resentment and anger that binds you to past experiences. This emotional release is essential for healing and allows you to reclaim your peace and move forward. When you hold on to grudges, the only person continually hurt is yourself as you relive the pain and let it color your current experiences and relationships. Understanding this dynamic is crucial, especially for those dealing with anxious attachment, as unresolved anger and hurt can intensify fears of abandonment and unworthiness.

Forgiveness can profoundly impact anxious attachment by loosening the grip of past hurts. It allows you to interact with the world and form new relationships without the heavy shadow of unresolved anger. For example, if you've been betrayed or let down in past relationships, your instinct might be to guard yourself against future pain by building walls around your emotions. However, this defense mechanism also blocks genuine intimacy and connection. By choosing to forgive, you are not opening yourself up to being hurt again; instead, you are healing the old wounds so they do not dictate your future interactions.

Approaching forgiveness requires a structured process, especially when the wounds are deep. Start by acknowledging the hurt. Fully recognize the impact of the actions or events on your life without minimizing or justifying them. This step is crucial—it's about permitting yourself to validate your feelings and affirming that it was not okay for you to be treated that way. Next, strive to understand the context of the situation or behavior. This doesn't mean excusing the behavior but rather understanding the complexities or factors that might have influenced it. Perhaps the person who hurt you acted out of their unresolved traumas or insecurities. This insight doesn't diminish your pain but can soften your anger, making it easier to overcome.

The most challenging step is consciously choosing to let go of grudges. It involves a deliberate decision to release the resentment and anger, not for the offender's sake but for your own healing. This choice often requires repeated effort; forgiveness is not a one-time act but a continuous process. If you begin slipping back into resentment, gently remind yourself of your decision to forgive. Over time, the emotional charge of the memories will fade, freeing you from the painful cycles of the past.

Self-forgiveness is also critical to this process, especially for those who blame themselves for past relationship traumas. It's not uncommon to harbor guilt or shame, believing somehow you could have prevented the hurt or chosen differently. Self-forgiveness involves recognizing that you did the best you could with the knowledge and resources available to you at the time. It's about treating yourself with the same compassion you would offer a friend, acknowledging your imperfections, and accepting that mistakes are part of growth. This acceptance is vital for healing and building healthier future relationships as it fosters a kinder and more understanding relationship with yourself.

Engaging in forgiveness, both of others and yourself, sets the stage for profound emotional healing. It shifts your focus from past grievances to present recovery and future peace, allowing you to engage more fully in life and open yourself to new, healthier relationships. As you continue to explore and apply forgiveness in your life, remember that each step toward forgiveness is a step toward freeing yourself from the chains of past hurts and reclaiming your emotional freedom.

6.4 Rebuilding Trust with Yourself and Others

In the aftermath of relationship trauma, the delicate fabric of trust is often torn, not just between you and others but within yourself. Understanding how to mend this fabric is essential for fostering secure attachments, whether with new partners, friends, or even with your own self-image. Rebuilding trust is not just about restoring faith in others; it's fundamentally about reconstructing your belief in your own judgment and reliability. This process, while intricate, is deeply rewarding as it gradually restores a sense of safety and openness in your interpersonal relationships.

Rebuilding trust in yourself is the cornerstone of this healing process. It starts with reaffirming your ability to trust your decisions and instincts. It might seem daunting if past choices led to pain, but it's important for moving forward. Begin by setting small, achievable commitments to yourself. These could be as simple as a daily walk, a set time for self-reflection, or maintaining a routine that nurtures your well-being. Each commitment fulfilled is a brick in the foundation of self-trust, proving to yourself that you are reliable and your decisions have value.

Additionally, setting realistic expectations for yourself is vital. Understand that healing and rebuilding trust is a gradual process; allow yourself the time and space to grow without the pressure of perfection. This approach fosters patience with yourself and alleviates the anxiety around making decisions, reinforcing your confidence in your ability to make healthy choices.

Honoring your needs and boundaries is paramount. After experiencing betrayal or disappointment, you might find it challenging to ask for what you need from relationships for fear of being seen as demanding or being disregarded again. However, clearly defining and respecting your boundaries is a testament to your self-respect and trust in your own needs. Start by identifying what feels safe and what doesn't and communicate these boundaries in your relationships. For example, if consistent communication is vital to you, express this need openly and observe how it is respected. This practice will reinforce your trust in your ability to protect and prioritize your needs and teach others how to interact with you, establishing mutual respect that is foundational for trust.

Extending trust to others is a gradual and careful process, especially when past experiences have left you wary. One effective way to rebuild this trust is by setting small, low-risk trust challenges. Engage in activities that require a degree of vulnerability but have low stakes, such as lending a book to a friend or sharing personal stories with a close colleague. Observe how they handle these situations. Do they return the book? Do they respect the confidentiality of your shared stories? These interactions prove their trustworthiness and help you gauge whether to extend deeper trust. Remember, trust is not about guaranteeing another's behavior but about being confident in your ability to handle their responses, whatever they may be.

Consistency and transparency in actions and communication are the threads that hold the fabric of trust together. In your interactions, strive to be as open and consistent as possible. You can keep your promises, communicate your feelings and thoughts honestly, and behave in predictable and reassuring ways to others. Simultaneously, expect and encourage the same from those around you. For instance, if you've agreed upon regular check-ins with a partner or friend, adhere to this arrangement diligently. If inconsistencies arise, address them openly rather than letting suspicions fester. This mutual commitment to consistency and transparency rebuilds trust and deepens the connection, creating a robust relationship where security and openness pave the way for lasting bonds.

As you navigate these steps, remember that rebuilding trust is an act of courage and commitment. It is about believing in the possibility of loyalty and integrity, both in yourself and others, despite past wounds. With each small step, each healed fragment of trust, you restore your faith in relationships and reclaim a more secure, connected, and open life.

6.5 Moving from Victim to Survivor

Shifting from seeing yourself as a victim to recognizing yourself as a survivor is a profound transformation. This change isn't just about semantics; it's about embracing a mindset that focuses on strength and resilience rather than vulnerability and suffering. When you view yourself as a survivor, you acknowledge your ability to overcome, learn from your experiences, and grow stronger because of them. This perspective empowers you, turning past traumas into sources of strength rather than perpetual wounds.

In this empowering transformation, knowledge plays a crucial role. Understanding the psychological impacts of your experiences, mainly how they have shaped your attachment style and influenced your relationship dynamics, gives you the tools to reconstruct your emotional outlook. Learning about different attachment styles, the effects of trauma on the brain and body, and the principles of trauma recovery can demystify your experiences and reduce feelings of isolation or confusion. For instance, recognizing that hypervigilance to relational cues is a typical response to trauma can help you make sense of your anxieties and guide you in developing healthier relational patterns. Armed with this knowledge, you're better prepared to tackle your healing process proactively, using informed strategies that enhance your resilience and self-efficacy.

Celebrating each step in your recovery process is vital in reinforcing your identity as a survivor. Recovery is rarely linear, composed instead of small victories and inevitable setbacks. By acknowledging and celebrating each positive step, no matter how small, you reinforce your progress and motivate yourself to continue. These celebrations could be as simple as acknowledging a day when you managed your triggers well or as significant as recognizing a shift in your relationship patterns. Each celebration is a reaffirmation of your strength and progress. It's a way to visually and emotionally mark your journey, seeing each success as a building block in your new life as a survivor.

Building a supportive network is also essential in this transformation. Surround yourself with people who recognize and affirm your survivor status. This network might include close friends who understand your journey, family members who support your growth, support groups, and therapists who provide empathy and insight. These relationships are vital, as they provide emotional support and reflect and reinforce your new identity as a survivor. They serve as mirrors, reflecting the strength and progress you might not always see in yourself. Furthermore, these relationships can provide practical support and feedback as you implement new coping strategies and relational patterns, making the journey less daunting.

As a survivor, your story is not defined by what has happened to you but by how you've moved forward. With each step, you move away from your past and toward a future where your experiences are sources of wisdom and strength. This chapter aims to assist you with the understanding and tools to make this shift, helping you weave your past experiences into the fabric of a richer, more resilient self.

As we conclude this chapter, remember that moving from victim to survivor is about overcoming past traumas and transforming them into foundations of strength and self-awareness. This shift is crucial for building healthier relationships and a more secure self-image. As you turn the page, carry the knowledge, strategies, and attitudes that can light your way, not just as someone who has survived but as someone who thrives.

Self-Assessment and Reflection Exercises for Chapter 6: Healing from Past Relationship Trauma

1. Mapping Personal History:

- Exercise: Create a timeline of your past significant relationships, noting key events, emotions, and outcomes. Identify any recurring patterns or triggers.
   - What do these patterns reveal about your attachment style and responses to trauma? How can understanding these patterns help you move forward?
   - This helps you visualize and understand the impact of past traumas on your current behaviors.

2. Recognizing Emotional Triggers:

- Exercise: Keep a daily log of situations that trigger strong emotional reactions. Detail what happened, how you felt, and how you responded.
    - After a week, review your log. What are the common triggers? How might these be linked to past traumas? How can you start addressing these triggers in healthier ways?
    - Tracking triggers can help you become more aware of them and start addressing them in healthier ways.

3. Journaling for Trigger Tracking:

- Exercise: Each time you experience a trigger, write a detailed journal entry about the event, your feelings, and any physical sensations.
    - What patterns emerge from your entries? How do your physical responses correspond with your emotional reactions? How can this awareness help you manage your triggers?
    - Journaling helps you process your emotions and identify patterns in your responses.

4. Engaging with Professional Assessments:

- Exercise: If possible, schedule a session with a therapist to explore deeply buried traumas and their impact on your current behavior.

After the session, write down any insights you gain. How can professional guidance complement your self-assessment and healing journey?

- Professional guidance can provide deeper insights and complement your self-assessment.

5. Forgiveness Practice:

- Exercise: Write a letter to someone who hurt you in the past, expressing your feelings and your journey toward forgiveness. You don't need to send it.
- How does expressing forgiveness make you feel? What steps can you take to let go of past hurts and move toward healing?
- Expressing forgiveness helps release lingering resentment and promotes healing.

6. Self-Forgiveness Exercise:

- Exercise: Write a compassionate letter to yourself, acknowledging past mistakes and expressing forgiveness and understanding.
- How does self-forgiveness impact your self-worth and ability to form healthy relationships? What steps can you take to reinforce this self-compassion?
- Self-forgiveness boosts self-worth and fosters healthier relationships.

7. Building Trust with Yourself and Others:

- Exercise: Set small, achievable commitments to yourself each week and follow through with them. Reflect on your ability to trust yourself and others.

- How does keeping commitments to yourself build self-trust? How can this practice improve your ability to trust others in your relationships?

- Keeping commitments to yourself builds self-trust, essential for trusting others.

By engaging in these exercises, you can start to unravel the impact of past relationship traumas, recognize and address emotional triggers, and build a path toward healing and healthier attachments.

Chapter Seven

Navigating Relationships with Avoidant and Disorganized Types

Imagine walking through a dense forest where the path ahead isn't always clear and the terrain changes unexpectedly. Much like this forest, relationships require us to navigate various landscapes, some more challenging than others. Particularly perplexing can be forming bonds with someone who embodies an avoidant attachment style—a journey that demands understanding and patience. This chapter illuminates the often misunderstood pathways of connecting with an avoidant partner, aiming to equip you with the insights and tools necessary to foster a loving, albeit complex, relationship dynamic.

7.1 Understanding the Avoidant Partner

Characterizing Avoidant Attachment

At the heart of avoidant attachment lies a paradoxical quest for emotional closeness and an intense fear of it. Typically, individuals with avoidant attachment styles treasure independence above all and often feel suffocated by too much closeness. They tend to withdraw under stress rather than seek support, a behavior that starkly contrasts with the anxious attachment style, where comfort is found through closer connections. Understanding these key traits is crucial; it's akin to learning the rules of a game where the stakes are the emotional well-being of both partners involved.

These individuals often create an aura of self-sufficiency, sometimes pushing others away just when they seem to be getting close. It can manifest in their propensity to focus excessively on work or hobbies or their habit of deflecting conversations that tread into the territory of deep emotional discussions. Recognizing these behaviors as protective mechanisms rather than personal rejections can transform your perspective and approach when dealing with an avoidant partner. It's about reading the signs posted along the trail, guiding you through the thicket of their emotional world.

Root Causes of Avoidant Behavior

The roots of avoidant attachment are often buried deep in the soil of one's upbringing and early relational experiences. Many avoidant individuals have histories of smothering relationships or interactions where a parent or caregiver stifled their independence. Alternatively, these caregivers could have been emotionally unavailable or unresponsive to the needs of the child. These caregivers might have discouraged closeness and intimacy, leading the child to learn to suppress their emotional needs. As a result, these children grow up believing they cannot rely on others for emotional support, teaching them to become self-reliant and avoid intimacy in relationships to protect themselves from potential rejection or disappointment. This ultimately cultivates a sense of lone self-reliance that makes depending on others feel unnervingly vulnerable. Understanding these root causes is not about excusing distant or detached behaviors but comprehending their origins. It's akin to understanding why the river you need to cross in your forest path flows so rapidly—not to hinder you but merely a natural consequence of its source.

Recognizing Avoidant Behaviors

To effectively navigate a relationship with an avoidant partner, you must become adept at recognizing the signs of their avoidance. These signs can be subtle or overt, ranging from changing the subject when the conversation gets too intimate to choosing to spend excessive time alone or at work rather than engaging in shared activities. These behaviors are their ways of maintaining a safe, controlled distance, a mechanism to protect themselves from the vulnerabilities that closeness can awaken.

Avoidant attachment styles are generally categorized into two subsets: dismissive-avoidant and fearful-avoidant. Individuals with a dismissive-avoidant style prioritize independence to the extent that they often dismiss the importance of close relationships and may appear emotionally distant or aloof. On the other hand, those with a fearful-avoidant style, also known as disorganized attachment, exhibit a mix of anxious and avoidant behaviors. They deeply crave emotional intimacy but simultaneously fear it, leading to unpredictable and often tumultuous relationship dynamics. Understanding these distinctions is useful for recognizing and addressing the unique challenges each style presents in relationships.

Emotional Effects on Partners

For someone with an anxious attachment style, being with an avoidant partner can sometimes feel like being adrift at sea—moments of calm interspersed with overwhelming waves of distress. The avoidant partner's withdrawal can trigger intense fears of abandonment and rejection in someone with an anxious attachment style. This dynamic can create a cycle of push and pull—a chase of sorts, where one partner advances in search of reassurance while the other retreats in search of space. Recognizing this pattern is the first step toward breaking the cycle. It allows you to respond to the behaviors and needs that drive them, fostering understanding and patience instead of frustration and despair.

Navigating a relationship with an avoidant partner requires a compass of deep understanding and acceptance. It's about recognizing the need for space as a deeply ingrained defense, not a personal affront. This understanding opens up pathways of communication that respect both partners' needs, helping to cultivate a relationship where both independence and intimacy can flourish. As you move forward in your relational journey, remember that every relationship terrain has challenges. Still, with the right tools and understanding, even the most complex paths can be navigated successfully.

7.2 Strategies for Engaging Disorganized Attachments

Disorganized attachment, often seen as the most complex attachment style, presents a unique challenge in relationships. It is characterized by a need for a coherent strategy in forming and maintaining attachments, resulting in behaviors that can seem contradictory and unpredictable. Individuals with this attachment style may oscillate between being overly clingy and distant, creating confusion and instability in their relationships. This inconsistency often stems from unresolved fears and conflicts related to intimacy—disorganized attachers crave closeness but are simultaneously scared of the vulnerability it entails. Understanding this chaotic inner landscape is pivotal in navigating a relationship with someone with disorganized attachment behaviors.

The internal conflicts experienced by those with disorganized attachment often arise from past traumas where caregivers were both sources of comfort and fear. Such conflicting experiences lead to mixed messages about the safety and reliability of close relationships. The fear of being too close can evoke anxiety about being engulfed or controlled, while the fear of being too distant can trigger panic about abandonment. These fears drive the seemingly contradictory behaviors that can bewilder partners who do not share the same attachment style. Recognizing these underlying fears helps us empathize with the disorganized individual's behavior, seeing them not as nonsensical or capricious but as a response to deep-seated fears.

When communicating with a partner who has a disorganized attachment style, maintaining a calm and consistent demeanor can be incredibly grounding for them. It's similar to being a steady anchor in choppy waters. Clear and direct communication to this attachment style also plays a crucial role. Ambiguities or subtleties in language can often be misinterpreted, feeding into their insecurities and fears. For instance, instead of saying, "Do you want to spend time together?" which could be ambiguous, you might say, "I would love to spend this evening together if you feel up to it." Clear communication reduces the chances for misunderstandings and provides a straightforward message that is easier for a disorganized individual to process without anxiety.

Creating Safety and Predictability

One of the most effective ways to manage a relationship with a disorganized partner is to establish a sense of safety and predictability. This doesn't mean creating a rigid schedule that stifles spontaneity; instead, it means building a relationship framework where actions and intentions are transparent, and routines are established that provide a sense of continuity and security. For example, regular check-ins at a certain time can create a predictable touchpoint to help alleviate anxiety about the relationship's stability. These check-ins can be as simple as a morning text message or a brief call on a lunch break, offering reassurance without being overbearing.

Creating a safe space allows the disorganized partner to express their fears and anxieties without judgment. This can create openness, facilitated through regular, structured conversations about the relationship where both partners can voice their needs and concerns. In these discussions, it is crucial to validate the partner's feelings regardless of how fluctuating or contradictory they may appear. This validation does not imply agreement but acknowledges their feelings as real and significant. It's also beneficial to develop and agree on strategies that address these fears, such as deciding on appropriate responses when one partner feels overwhelmed by closeness or needs reassurance due to fear of abandonment.

Navigating a relationship with someone who has a disorganized attachment style requires patience, understanding, and a proactive approach to communication and reassurance. By striving to understand the chaos of their internal world, maintaining clear and consistent communication, and creating a relationship environment characterized by safety and predictability, you can build a bridge to a more secure and stable connection. This approach supports your partner's attachment needs and fosters a deeper understanding and bond between you both, transforming the unpredictable currents of disorganized attachment into navigable waters.

7.3 Maintaining Your Emotional Balance

In the intricacies of relationships, especially those marked by complex attachment styles, maintaining your emotional equilibrium isn't just beneficial—it's necessary. Think of yourself as a gardener tending to your garden; just as plants need the right balance of sunlight, water, and nutrients to thrive, you need a balance of self-care, healthy boundaries, and emotional self-sufficiency to maintain your well-being in relationships. Self-care is your sunlight, essential for growth and vitality. It encompasses practices that nourish your body, soul, and mind. It might mean setting aside time for activities you love which help you reconnect with yourself and disengage from the stressors of relationship dynamics. It also involves more reflective practices such as meditation or yoga, strengthening your physical being and bringing clarity and peace to your mind. Prioritizing these activities can help you remain centered and calm even when relationship challenges loom large.

Setting healthy boundaries is your water, crucial for sustaining your growth without becoming overwhelmed. In the context of relationships, boundaries help you define where your limits lie and how much emotional input and output you can handle. This is especially important when dealing with partners who might not fully meet your emotional needs or whose attachment behaviors might trigger your anxieties. For example, if you find that constant texting with a partner stirs anxiety, setting a boundary around communication can help manage your stress. Communicate clearly with your partner about your needs—perhaps agreeing on specific times to catch up during the day instead of constant messaging. Establishing these boundaries helps prevent resentment and emotional exhaustion, as it ensures you are not overextending yourself emotionally and are interacting in a way that preserves your emotional well-being.

Developing emotional self-sufficiency is your essential nutrient mix, enriching your ability to stand alone without constant external validation. In relationships, this means cultivating a strong sense of self that does not depend solely on your partner's mood or actions for stability. It involves building self-confidence and self-compassion to support yourself emotionally, regardless of external circumstances. Techniques such as positive self-talk, where you encourage and affirm yourself, can fortify your self-esteem and reduce dependency on others for emotional satisfaction. For instance, replacing thoughts of "I am not loved enough" with "I am worthy of love and I love myself" can significantly alter your emotional landscape, making you less reliant on others' actions to feel valued and secure.

Mindfulness and emotional regulation are your tools for pruning and keeping your garden in order, ensuring no part grows too wild or withers. Mindfulness helps you stay rooted in the present moment, enhancing your awareness of your emotional state and thought patterns. This heightened awareness can be incredibly empowering in managing your responses to relationship dynamics. When you observe your emotions without judgment, you can better control them rather than let them control you. Techniques such as deep breathing or mindful walking engage your senses and focus your mind, pulling you away from ruminating on past conflicts or future worries. Additionally, practices in emotional regulation, such as the 'stop, breathe, reflect, choose' technique, empower you to handle emotional upheavals more effectively. When faced with a challenging situation, pause to stop and breathe deeply, reflect on what you are feeling, and then choose how to respond in a way that aligns with your emotional health goals.

Through these practices—self-care, setting healthy boundaries, cultivating emotional self-sufficiency, and engaging in mindfulness and emotional regulation—you equip yourself with the necessary tools to maintain your emotional balance. Like the gardener who nurtures their garden with the right balance of sunlight, water, and nutrients, you too can nurture your emotional well-being, ensuring that you remain strong, centered, and flourishing regardless of the complexities of your relationships. This approach enhances personal growth and enriches relationships, creating a healthier, more balanced connection with yourself and those you care about.

7.4 When to Hold On and When to Let Go

In the intricate dance of relationships, knowing when to hold on and when it's time to release gracefully is a profound skill akin to understanding the rhythm of music. It's about sensing the beats of joy and discord and deciding whether the music still brings enough pleasure or if it's time to change the tune. Assessing the overall health of your relationship involves a deep and honest look at various facets, including mutual respect, satisfaction, and personal growth. Imagine this assessment as a health check-up for your relationship where both partners' emotional, mental, and physical contributions are examined.

Start by reflecting on the level of mutual respect in your relationship. Respect is the soil in which love grows; it's fundamental. Ask yourself if you feel valued for who you are, not just for what you do or how you make your partner feel. Does your partner listen to you, acknowledge your feelings, and consider your views, even when disagreeing? Consider how conflicts are handled: are they resolved through understanding and compromise, or do they leave scars of resentment? Mutual respect ensures the roots remain intact even during storms, holding the relationship steady.

Next, evaluate the satisfaction each of you derives from the relationship. Satisfaction in this context goes beyond momentary happiness; it's about feeling content and secure in the relationship's ongoing state. It's about knowing that your emotional needs are met and that you feel better for having your partner. Reflect on the times you spend together: do they lift you, leaving you feeling better about yourself and your life? Or do they often result in feelings of frustration or emptiness? Satisfaction gauges the relationship's health, indicating whether the emotional environment is nurturing or neglectful.

Personal growth is another crucial area to assess. A healthy relationship promotes an environment where both partners can grow and evolve. It supports your ambitions and celebrates your successes. Consider whether you feel supported in pursuing your personal goals and interests. Does the relationship challenge you in positive ways, encouraging you to grow and learn, or does it hold you back, making you feel like you are stuck? Relationships should be catalysts for personal development, inspiring you to expand rather than constrict your sense of self.

Recognizing toxic or destructive patterns is essential in deciding whether to hold on or let go. These patterns might manifest as persistent unhappiness, disrespect, or even emotional abuse. Signs to watch for include:

- **Lack of Trust**: A constant lack of trust, with accusations, jealousy, or spying, indicates deep issues in the relationship.

- **Disrespect for Boundaries**: Ignoring personal, emotional, or physical boundaries is a serious red flag. Partners in a healthy relationship respect each other's limits.

- **Emotional or Physical Abuse**: Any form of abuse, whether emotional, verbal, or physical, is a clear sign to leave the relationship immediately.

- **Constant Criticism**: If your partner frequently belittles or criticizes you, undermining your self-esteem, it's a major warning sign.

- **Gaslighting**: If your partner makes you question your reality or feelings, consistently denies their wrongdoings, or manipulates you into doubting your sanity, it's a serious red flag.

- **Control and Manipulation**: Toxic behavior occurs when your partner tries to control your actions, decisions, or social interactions or manipulates situations to get their way.

- **Lack of Support or Empathy**: If your partner shows little interest in your feelings, achievements, or struggles and lacks empathy or support, it indicates a significant problem.

It's essential to be honest with yourself about the presence and impact of these behaviors. They often serve as significant indicators that the relationship is not just unhealthy but potentially damaging. Evaluating whether to stay or leave involves recognizing the negatives and weighing them against the potential for change. Engage in open and honest communication with your partner about your concerns. This conversation can be a turning point, revealing whether there is a commitment to mutual growth and healing. Sometimes, the decision to part ways might be the most loving choice if it leads to healthier, happier lives apart.

Several strategies can aid those facing the difficult decision to hold on or let go. Consulting with trusted friends or therapists can provide new perspectives and emotional support. Journaling about your feelings and fears can offer insights into your emotional patterns and clarify your thoughts. Taking time for self-reflection is crucial; it allows you to listen to your inner voice and discern what is truly best for your emotional and mental well-being.

Navigating the decision to hold on or let go is always challenging. It requires courage, honesty, and self-awareness. Remember, every relationship teaches us something valuable, whether we choose to stay and grow together or part ways with respect and love. By approaching this crossroads with a clear mind and compassionate heart, you empower yourself to make the choice that aligns with your deepest needs and values, guiding you toward authentic happiness and fulfillment.

7.5 Building Bridges: Developing Mutual Understanding and Respect

Understanding the journey of relationships often means learning to move in sync with someone whose steps differ from yours. This synchronization doesn't necessarily come naturally; it requires a deliberate effort to foster empathy, patience, and respect. Together, these elements form the cornerstone of a strong and enduring relationship, especially when partners have differing attachment styles.

Empathy, the ability to understand and share the feelings of another, is particularly crucial. It goes beyond mere sympathy to deeply understanding your partner's inner emotional world. Developing empathy for your partner's attachment style involves actively listening to their fears and motivations without judgment.

For instance, if your partner has an avoidant attachment style, they might fear losing their independence within the relationship. Here, empathy allows you to understand why they might cherish solitude, not as a rejection but as a vital part of their self-expression. Techniques to foster this empathy include open-ended conversations in which you explore each other's past experiences and how they shape your current behaviors. These discussions should be approached with curiosity rather than an agenda, aiming to truly understand rather than to correct or convince.

Patience and respect are equally vital in dealing with differences in attachment styles. Patience allows you to give your partner the time they need to change and adjust without forcing them to rush their emotional processes. It's about providing the seed time to sprout; not all growth happens at a visible pace. On the other hand, respect involves honoring your partner's needs and boundaries as valid even when they differ from yours. It means not trivializing their feelings or pushing them beyond what they're comfortable with. For example, if a partner feels overwhelmed by too much closeness, respecting their need for space—even when it's hard—underscores their autonomy and your mutual respect.

Joint problem-solving is an effective way to bridge differences and foster a collaborative spirit within the relationship. This approach involves both partners actively finding solutions to issues that respect their individual needs. It could be as simple as negotiating how much time to spend together versus apart or how to handle disagreements in a way that doesn't trigger a fear response in either partner. The key here is to view these challenges as a team effort, not a battleground for individual interests. Techniques such as setting a regular 'relationship check-in' where both partners can bring up issues in a non-confrontational setting can be incredibly beneficial. These meetings should focus on understanding each other's perspectives and working together toward a solution that considers both partners' well-being.

Celebrating differences rather than viewing them as obstacles can dramatically transform relationship dynamics. Every individual brings unique traits, experiences, and perspectives that can enrich a relationship, offering personal and relational growth opportunities. For example, an avoidant partner's need for independence can encourage an anxious partner to explore their own hobbies and interests, fostering a greater sense of self and autonomy. Similarly, an anxious partner's capacity for deep emotional connections can help an avoidant partner explore the richness of closer emotional engagements. Embracing these differences as gifts rather than barriers deepens the relationship and contributes to a richer, more diverse experience for both partners.

Building bridges across different attachment styles is not about changing who you or your partner truly are.. It's about developing a deeper understanding, respect, and appreciation for each other's differences and working together to create a relationship that honors both partners fully. As you integrate these strategies into your relationship, you'll find that the bridges you build connect you more deeply with your partner and enrich your emotional landscape, offering new ways of understanding and connection.

As we wrap up this exploration of developing mutual understanding and respect, remember that the strength of a relationship lies not in its perfection but in its capacity to transform challenges into opportunities for growth and deeper connection. The techniques and perspectives discussed here are tools for navigating differences and stepping stones to a more compassionate, empathic, and fulfilling relationship. In the next chapter, we will delve into the advanced strategies for relationship success, building on the foundation of understanding and respect to explore deeper levels of connection and love.

Self-Assessment and Reflection Exercises for Chapter 7: Navigating Relationships with Avoidant and Disorganized Types

1. Understanding the Avoidant Partner:

- Exercise: Reflect on your relationship with an avoidant partner. Write about specific instances where their need for space made you feel anxious or insecure. Consider how you responded and how it affected your relationship.
- This exercise helps you identify response patterns and understand how your partner's behavior impacts your emotions.

2. Creating Safety and Predictability:

Exercise: Develop a plan to introduce more predictability and safety into your relationship. This could include setting regular communication times or planning regular activities together.
- This helps to create a structured environment that reduces anxiety and fosters a sense of security.

3. Role-Playing Scenarios:

Exercise: With a trusted friend or therapist, role-play scenarios in which you navigate conflicts with your avoidant or disorganized partner. Practice responding calmly and assertively.

- Role-playing prepares you for real-life situations, allowing you to practice and refine your responses in a safe setting.

4. Empathy and Patience Practice:

Exercise: Commit to practicing empathy and patience with your partner. Each day, note one instance where you listened without judgment and showed understanding toward their behavior.

- This exercise fosters a deeper emotional connection and improves your ability to respond supportively to your partner's needs.

5. Setting Healthy Boundaries:

- Exercise: Identify areas in your relationship where boundaries are needed to protect your emotional well-being. Write down clear, respectful boundaries and discuss them with your partner.
 - Setting boundaries helps maintain your emotional health and ensures that both partners' needs are respected.

6. Self-Care Routine:

- Exercise: Develop a self-care routine that helps you manage anxiety and maintain your emotional balance. This might include activities like exercise, meditation, or spending time with friends.
 - A consistent self-care routine supports your overall well-being and helps manage stress and anxiety.

7. Professional Support:

- Exercise: Consider seeking professional support individually or as a couple. Make an appointment with a therapist who specializes in attachment issues.
 - Professional guidance can provide tailored strategies and deeper insights into improving your relationship dynamics.

These exercises aim to help you better understand your relationship dynamics, develop strategies to manage anxiety and foster healthier interactions with avoidant and disorganized partners. Engaging in these activities can create a more balanced and fulfilling relationship for you and your partner.

Chapter Eight

Advanced Strategies for Relationship Success

I magine you're curating a rich forest where each season brings a new depth of color and experience; this is like nurturing a long-term relationship. Over time, the initial seeds of attraction may grow into deep roots of commitment, but the continued flourishing of this love requires understanding, especially in the realm of attachment styles. This chapter delves into the attachment patterns in relationships. It explores their pivotal role in long-term satisfaction and provides strategies to cultivate a thriving partnership that can stand the test of time.

8.1 The Role of Attachment in Long-Term Relationship Satisfaction

Exploring Attachment Stability

Initially formed in early childhood, attachment styles profoundly influence how we interact in romantic relationships. However, these styles are not set in stone; they can evolve with conscious effort and significant relationships. Over time, an individual with an anxious attachment style can experience shifts toward more secure attachment behaviors, particularly when involved with a supportive partner who provides consistent affection and reassurance. Similarly, those with an avoidant attachment style might open up more as trust and safety within the relationship are established.

The transformation of attachment styles hinges on numerous factors, including the dynamics of the relationship itself, individual growth, and external pressures such as career demands or family obligations. For instance, the arrival of children might prompt a deeper security in one partner while causing another to confront unresolved attachment issues. Understanding that these styles can evolve helps both partners remain adaptable and responsive to each other's changing emotional landscapes, fostering a resilient bond that nurtures mutual growth and fulfillment.

Attachment and Relationship Satisfaction

Secure attachment underpins the most satisfying long-term relationships. It fosters an environment where trust, mutual respect, and emotional availability are the norms. Securely attached individuals are better equipped to provide the emotional support that nurtures happiness in relationships. They tend to approach conflicts as tasks to solve together rather than arenas in which to prove themselves right. This collaborative approach to problem-solving not only smooths over potential conflicts but also deepens the intimacy between partners, as each conflict resolution becomes an opportunity to understand and love each other better.

Linking theory to practice, securely attached partners often use their relationship as a secure base from which to explore the world, both literally and metaphorically. This security allows them to pursue personal goals and hobbies, which enrich their individual lives and bring interesting experiences and energies back into the relationship, keeping the romance and intrigue alive.

Mitigating Attachment Insecurity

For those grappling with insecure attachment styles—whether anxious, avoidant, or disorganized—there are effective strategies to foster more security within the relationship. Communication is vital; regularly sharing feelings and reassurances can help soothe an anxious partner's fears of abandonment, while consistently respecting boundaries can help an avoidant partner feel safe enough to engage more deeply.

Therapeutic interventions can also play a crucial role. Couples therapy and individual therapy can provide insights and tools to understand and improve one's attachment style. Practices such as 'earned secure attachment'—understanding one's past and how actively choosing different behaviors can develop a secure attachment style—are particularly beneficial. This proactive approach allows individuals to rewrite their relational scripts, transforming their interactions and stability within the relationship.

Case Studies of Long-lasting Relationships

Consider the story of Elena and Jane, a couple from backgrounds of anxious and avoidant attachments, respectively. Initially, their relationship was a roller coaster of closeness and distance, with Elena constantly seeking reassurance and Jane pulling away in need of space. However, through mutual efforts to understand their attachment styles and engage in couples therapy, they learned to navigate their needs effectively. Jane began to understand the importance of small gestures of reassurance for Elena, and Elena worked on self-soothing techniques during Jane's need for solitude. Over time, their mindful efforts helped them develop a more secure attachment with each other, leading to increased relationship satisfaction and resilience against typical relationship stressors.

In another example, consider Maya and Tom, who both had histories of disorganized attachments due to turbulent childhood experiences. Misunderstandings and intense emotional reactions marked their early relationship. However, their commitment to healing led them to engage in joint and individual therapy sessions where they learned to identify their triggers and communicate their feelings more clearly. This hard work allowed them to support each other's healing, gradually building a stable and loving relationship that allowed them to enjoy parenting their two children despite their challenging attachment histories.

These stories highlight that understanding, patience, and consistent effort can transform insecure attachment styles and foster long-lasting relationship satisfaction. By actively working on understanding and adapting to each other's attachment needs, couples can create a loving environment that promotes mutual happiness and growth, proving that even misunderstandings and relational anxieties can be nurtured into places of beauty and tranquility.

8.2 Advanced Empathy Skills for Deepening Intimacy

Empathy, in its most profound sense, goes beyond merely understanding or sharing the feelings of another. It involves a deep, intuitive sense of another's emotional world—a skill that, when mastered, can profoundly deepen intimacy and strengthen bonds in any relationship. Advanced empathy, or empathic accuracy, is akin to tuning an instrument to ensure it plays in harmony with others; it involves attuning to your partner's subtle emotional cues and understanding their thoughts and feelings at a nuanced level. Consider, for example, the difference between hearing that your partner had a bad day and understanding the specific emotional undertones—whether they feel overwhelmed, unappreciated, or perhaps disconnected. This deeper insight allows you to respond in a way that directly addresses their emotional state, thereby deepening your connection and trust.

Building this level of empathy requires active listening and observation, heightened by a genuine curiosity about your partner's inner world. It's about noticing the slight tremor in their voice that hints at anxiety or the fleeting look of disappointment quickly masked by a smile. Such keen observation allows you to ask more pointed, thoughtful questions that encourage your partner to open up and share their true feelings. This practice not only conveys that you care deeply but also that you are invested in understanding their experiences as fully as possible. Over time, this builds a foundation of trust and safety, where both partners feel deeply seen and understood, paving the way for a more intimate and fulfilling relationship.

Emotional attunement takes this concept a step further by synchronizing your emotional responses with those of your partner. This synchronization isn't merely mirroring emotions; it's about harmonizing your emotional responses so that you both feel emotionally connected and supported. For instance, if your partner is excited about a new opportunity, you share in their excitement, not just superficially, but genuinely engaging with their happiness and reinforcing the joy it brings them. On the flip side, during times of stress or sadness, your calm and steady presence can provide comfort and stability. Achieving this level of attunement requires you to be emotionally present and responsive, which fosters a deep sense of companionship and togetherness.

Practicing vulnerability is integral to this process. Vulnerability allows for the openness required for deep emotional connections to form. It involves sharing your own fears, desires, and weaknesses, thereby setting a tone of openness and authenticity in the relationship. This mutual exchange of vulnerability fosters a profound intimacy, as both partners feel safe enough to shed their protective layers and share their true selves. Empathy here is crucial—it creates the safe space needed for such openness. When you respond to your partner's vulnerabilities with empathy and support, you reinforce their trust in you and encourage a deeper emotional connection that makes the relationship more resilient and rewarding.

Advanced empathy can be transformative in conflicts, which are inevitable in any relationship. Often, conflicts escalate because partners respond more to the surface issues rather than the emotional underpinnings of the disagreement. Empathy lets you discern the emotions driving your partner's behavior, often revealing the real issues at play. Understanding these emotional underpinnings allows you to address the core of the conflict more effectively and compassionately. For instance, if a partner expresses anger over your spending habits, empathy might reveal their real concern is security and future stability, not simply the money spent. Addressing this underlying fear can turn a potential argument into a constructive discussion about shared values and future goals, deepening understanding and cooperation in the relationship.

Deploying these advanced empathy skills— emotional attunement, practicing vulnerability, and empathy in conflict resolution—cultivates a relationship environment where trust, intimacy, and mutual respect flourish. As these elements become woven into the fabric of your relationship, they enhance everyday interactions and fortify your bond against the inevitable challenges ahead, creating a resilient, loving partnership that enriches both of your lives.

8.3 Negotiating Needs and Desires in Mature Relationships

In a long-term relationship, balancing individual needs with shared goals is both an art and a necessity.

Picture this: two chefs working together in the same kitchen, each with their own favorite ingredients and cooking styles. For the meal to succeed, they must find a way to honor both their individual tastes and the overall vision for their shared dish. Similarly, ensuring both partners feel valued and heard requires ongoing communication and flexibility. It begins with each person clearly understanding their own needs. Whether it's the need for alone time, social interaction, or shared hobbies, recognizing and respecting these individual needs helps prevent resentment and disconnection. The next step involves openly discussing these needs with your partner. This isn't just about stating what you want but engaging in a dialogue that explores how both partners' needs can be met. For instance, if one partner needs more quiet time at home while the other thrives on hosting gatherings, they might agree on designated nights for hosting friends and quiet evenings.

Negotiating desires within a relationship often requires a delicate balance of give and take. It's about finding common ground where both partners can be satisfied without feeling that they are sacrificing more than they are comfortable with. This negotiation may look like choosing a vacation combining adventure for one and relaxation for the other or alternating who chooses the movie on movie night. The key here is mutual respect for each other's desires and finding creative ways to meet in the middle that are enjoyable for both. It's also vital for each person to remain open to adjusting their expectations and be willing to explore new things that might initially be outside their comfort zone.

The stakes are often higher when aligning long-term goals; the negotiations, whether career paths, family planning, or personal growth, can become more complex. Openly discussing these goals, perhaps during a dedicated "relationship check-in" or planning session, can prevent misalignments that might lead to conflicts. During these discussions, it's important to talk about what each goal entails and why they are important to each person. Understanding the 'why' behind a partner's goals fosters empathy and support. For example, if one partner wants to move to a new city for a job opportunity, discussing the career benefits and how this move could improve their quality of life and sense of fulfillment can help the other partner see the value in the change. If differences in long-term goals are identified, finding ways to compromise or support each other's goals without resentment is crucial. This might involve one partner taking the lead on a certain goal while the other provides support, then switching roles for another goal.

Periodically renegotiating the terms of your relationship as both of you grow and evolve is also crucial. What worked for you both five years ago might hold different relevance today. These renegotiations can cover changes in daily routines, financial planning, or emotional support systems. They provide an opportunity to reset expectations and ensure both partners feel content and valued. For instance, after a career change, a couple might need to renegotiate their financial contributions to household expenses or discuss how to manage time so that both partners can still spend quality time together despite differing schedules.

Navigating these relationship aspects requires open communication, empathy, and a willingness to make adjustments. By actively engaging in these practices, partners can ensure that their relationship survives and thrives, adapting to each phase of life with resilience and mutual respect. This ongoing dialogue helps build a dynamic and responsive partnership deeply rooted in a mutual understanding and appreciation of each other's evolving needs and dreams.

8.4 The Impact of Life Transitions on Attachment Styles

Life, with its constant ebb and flow, brings about transitions that test the fabric of our relationships and, inherently, our attachment styles. Key life transitions such as becoming parents, career changes, significant birthdays, or even the evolution from one phase of life to another, like retirement, can unsettle the established patterns of interaction between partners. These transitions push individuals and their relationships into new territories, often creating profound shifts in attachment behaviors. For instance, the transition to parenthood can intensify an anxious attachment style due to new vulnerabilities and responsibilities, or it may lead to a more secure attachment as partners rely more deeply on each other for support.

Handling these transitions successfully requires a conscious effort to adapt attachment behaviors so that the relationship survives and thrives. This adaptation might look like an avoidant partner choosing to engage more openly with their feelings and share the emotional load during a partner's career transition, which inherently involves uncertainties and stress. Similarly, an anxiously attached individual might need to practice self-reliance and patience when their partner is navigating personal challenges such as health issues or the loss of a loved one.

Implementing strategies such as scheduled check-ins can foster communication and provide regular updates on each partner's emotional state, helping to mitigate misunderstandings or feelings of neglect during busy or challenging times. Additionally, setting aside time for relationship-building activities that reinforce the partnership, like date nights or weekend getaways, can help maintain the emotional connection, ensuring that both partners feel valued and prioritized despite the external changes.

Support systems play a critical role during these transitions, providing an external buffer that can help absorb some of the stress. Friends, family members, or professional counselors can offer emotional support and practical help, which can be particularly crucial during transitions like the arrival of a new child or a move to a new city. For instance, grandparents or close friends can provide childcare, allowing the couple time to reconnect and support each other. A professional counselor can offer strategies and a space to discuss how to manage anxieties related to a job loss or change.

Building resilience in the face of these transitions is crucial. It allows couples to navigate through changes without losing the essence of their relationship, and it can be cultivated through proactive communication, mutual support, and flexibility in facing new situations. Resilience involves recognizing that each transition is a phase that holds possibilities for growth and deeper understanding. For example, a couple facing the empty nest phase can choose to see this as an opportunity to rediscover each other and explore new interests together. Similarly, navigating a career change can become an avenue for exploring new aspects of your personality and abilities, which your partner can share and support, adding a layer of richness to the relationship.

In each situation, the key lies in viewing transitions not as threats but as opportunities to strengthen the relationship. By maintaining open lines of communication, supporting each other emotionally, and adapting to new roles and situations, couples can ensure that their relationship not only withstands the challenges of life transitions but also emerges stronger and more connected. This approach transforms potential stressors into stepping stones for building a deeper, more resilient union anchored in understanding, flexibility, and mutual support.

8.5 Cultivating a Shared Growth Mindset

Within the landscape of relationship dynamics, embracing a growth mindset can be likened to nurturing a garden that you and your partner tend together, believing that it will flourish and thrive with care and persistence.

Adopting a shared growth mindset can transform how you and your partner respond to the inevitable challenges that relationships face. It fosters a proactive approach to problem-solving and personal development, which fortifies your relationship against the strains of everyday stressors and deeper issues. For instance, when conflicts arise, instead of viewing them through a lens of criticism or avoidance, you see them as a chance to enhance your understanding of each other, deepen your communication skills, and strengthen your bond. This perspective encourages both partners to remain engaged and motivated even when navigating difficult discussions because you regard these situations as growth opportunities.

Moreover, a growth mindset can significantly boost the capacity for empathy and patience between partners. It allows for a more compassionate space where mistakes are not seen as failures but as part of the learning and growing process. This environment supports open dialogue about each other's needs and vulnerabilities, which is crucial for mutual support and understanding. For example, suppose one partner struggles with feelings of inadequacy in their professional life. In that case, the other can help reframe these feelings as typical aspects of personal development, encouraging a focus on progress and learning rather than on perceived shortcomings.

To effectively foster mutual personal development, it is beneficial to set aside regular times for discussion about each other's goals and aspirations. During these conversations, actively listen to one another's thoughts and supportively respond to them, reinforcing your shared values and the commitment to grow together. Engaging in activities both partners find enriching—such as taking a class together, reading a book, or even engaging in a new hobby—can also be powerful. These shared activities provide fun and learning and create shared experiences that can bring you closer and deepen your connection.

Celebrating growth milestones is equally important in nurturing a culture of appreciation and mutual support within the relationship. Whether it's acknowledging small steps like successfully managing a week full of stress without conflict or significant achievements like reaching a personal goal of fitness or education, recognizing and celebrating these milestones can greatly enhance the sense of team spirit within your relationship. It reminds both partners that growth is ongoing and that each effort, no matter the size, contributes to strengthening the relationship. Regularly reflecting on how far you have come, individually and as a couple, can also be incredibly affirming and motivating. It serves as a reminder of the dynamic capability of your partnership to adapt, evolve, and thrive through all of life's challenges.

In this garden of growth, every effort you make, and every challenge you overcome enriches the soil of your relationship, making it more fertile and robust. By committing to a mindset that values growth and by actively supporting each other in your personal and joint endeavors, you cultivate a relationship that is not only enduring but also vibrant and fulfilling. This approach doesn't just prepare you to handle future challenges; it transforms the very fabric of your relationship into one marked by continual learning, mutual support, and ever-deepening love.

Moving Forward

As we wrap up this exploration of cultivating a shared growth mindset, remember that the essence of this approach lies in embracing change and challenges as integral to your shared journey. It's about celebrating each step of growth, supporting each other unconditionally, and striving to become better partners. As you turn to the next chapter, carry forward this mindset and let it infuse all aspects of your relationship, ensuring that your bond survives and thrives, regardless of what life may bring.

Self-Assessment and Reflection Exercises for Chapter 8: Advanced Strategies for Relationship Success

1. Attachment Stability and Relationship Satisfaction:

 - Exercise: Reflect on a recent conflict in your relationship. How did you and your partner approach resolving it? Identify one strategy from this chapter that could have improved the outcome and plan how you might use it in the future.

   Understanding how secure attachment can transform conflict resolution, this exercise helps you approach future disagreements collaboratively, deepening trust and satisfaction in your relationship.

2. Empathy Skills for Deepening Intimacy:

- Exercise: Think about a time when you misunderstood your partner's feelings or needs. How did you initially respond? Write down how you could have used advanced empathy skills to understand and support them better.

- Reflecting on past misunderstandings and considering how advanced empathy could have helped enhances your ability to connect deeply and respond thoughtfully in future interactions.

3. Negotiating Needs and Desires:

- Exercise: List three needs or desires you have in your relationship that haven't been fully met. Discuss with your partner how to negotiate to meet these needs while respecting theirs.

- Engaging in open discussions about unmet needs fosters mutual respect and helps balance both partners' desires, contributing to a healthier and more satisfying relationship dynamic.

4. Managing Life Transitions:

- Exercise: Identify a recent or upcoming life transition (e.g., moving, career change, having a child). Discuss with your partner how you can support each other during this period, incorporating strategies from this chapter.

- Preparing together for significant life changes strengthens your partnership, ensuring that you both feel supported and resilient during times of transition.

5. Cultivating a Shared Growth Mindset:

 - Exercise: Set a joint goal with your partner related to personal or relationship growth (e.g., learning a new skill, improving communication). Create a plan to achieve this goal, including steps you will take and how you will support each other.

 - Setting and working towards shared goals reinforces a growth mindset, encouraging continuous development and mutual support in your relationship.

These exercises help you integrate the advanced strategies discussed in this chapter into your daily life, fostering a more secure and fulfilling partnership.

Chapter Nine

Special Considerations in Anxious Attachment

In the digital age, how we connect with others has transformed dramatically, weaving technology into the fabric of our interpersonal relationships. This evolution brings with it a unique set of challenges and opportunities, especially for those grappling with anxious attachment. As you navigate the complex web of digital communication, understanding its impact on your attachment style can empower you to foster healthier, more fulfilling connections.

9.1 Anxious Attachment in Digital Communication and Social Media

Impact of Digital Communication on Anxious Attachment

The immediacy and permanence of digital communication have reshaped the landscape of relationships, offering instant connectivity and introducing new triggers for anxious attachers. Text messages and social media platforms become arenas where anxieties can flourish—each unread message or ambiguous emoji can seem like a puzzle to be solved. Suppose you are overanalyzing digital interactions or feeling a knot in your stomach when a reply doesn't come quickly. In that case, you're experiencing firsthand how digital communication can amplify anxious attachment behaviors.

This heightened alertness stems from the digital world's lack of non-verbal cues. Unlike face-to-face interactions, where body language and tone of voice provide context, digital communications are stark, leaving much to interpretation. For someone with anxious attachment, this ambiguity can turn every paused conversation or 'seen' message into a source of worry and speculation. The permanence of digital messages also plays a role—texts and emails can be revisited and overanalyzed, sometimes feeding into a cycle of anxiety and misunderstanding.

Setting Boundaries Online

To mitigate these challenges, setting boundaries in your digital interactions is vital. This involves more than just limiting screen time—it's about creating guidelines that protect your emotional well-being. Start by defining specific times during the day to check social media or respond to non-urgent texts. For instance, you might only check your messages during lunch and after dinner. This structured approach can prevent the compulsive checking that often triggers anxiety.

Additionally, adjusting notification settings can significantly reduce anxiety. Turn off non-essential notifications so that you're not constantly pulled back into the digital world by every ping. Choose to engage on your terms when you are mentally prepared and less vulnerable to misinterpretation or emotional upheaval. These boundaries aren't about isolating yourself but about taking control of your digital interactions so that they serve you, not your anxieties.

Positive Use of Digital Tools

Despite its challenges, digital communication offers tools to harness and strengthen relationships and manage anxious attachment effectively. Scheduled communication, for example, can be a gift for those with anxious attachment. Agreeing on regular check-in times with your partner or close friends can provide reassurance and reduce the uncertainty that fuels anxiety. These scheduled interactions ensure that communication remains consistent and predictable, providing a sense of security in the relationship.

Another positive strategy is using direct and clear language in your digital communications. Be explicit about your feelings and needs rather than assuming the other person knows what you mean. This clarity can prevent misunderstandings that might otherwise escalate anxiety. For example, if you're feeling overwhelmed and need space, a clear message explaining your feelings can help your partner understand your needs without guessing or misinterpreting.

Digital Etiquette

Understanding and practicing good digital etiquette is crucial for maintaining healthy online interactions, especially for those with anxious attachments. Digital etiquette encompasses several practices, but the key among them is clarity in communication. Always aim to communicate clearly and kindly, avoiding vague language that could be misinterpreted. Be prompt in your responses where possible, or let the other person know if you will be delayed in replying. This kind of predictability and transparency can significantly reduce anxiety for both parties involved.

Moreover, educating yourself and others about the impact of digital communication on mental health can foster more empathetic interactions. Recognize that behind every screen is someone who might interpret messages through their own filter of anxieties and experiences. Promoting a culture of kindness and understanding in digital interactions contributes to a healthier, more supportive online environment.

As you continue to navigate the digital world, remember that the tools and platforms themselves are not inherently anxiety-inducing—it's how we use them that determines their impact on our lives and attachments. By setting thoughtful boundaries, using digital tools positively, and practicing respectful digital etiquette, you can transform your online interactions into sources of support and reassurance rather than stress and uncertainty.

9.2 Dealing with Infidelity and Anxious Reactions

For individuals grappling with anxious attachment, the fear of infidelity can loom large, casting doubt in relationships that might otherwise feel secure. The core of anxious attachment—fear of abandonment and a strong need for reassurance—can sometimes skew perceptions, making the threat of infidelity feel ever-present. This heightened sensitivity can stem from past experiences of broken trust or from an intrinsic fear that they are not enough to keep a partner fully committed. Understanding how to navigate these fears without letting them dominate your relationship is crucial in this complex emotional space.

When suspicions of infidelity enter a relationship, they can ignite a storm of emotions. If you find yourself wrestling with these worries, it's important to approach them carefully to avoid the destructive cycle of accusations and counteraccusations that can arise from anxious impulses. Begin by examining the foundation of your suspicions. Are they driven by specific behaviors you've observed or are they more a reflection of your insecurities? Communicating these feelings with your partner can be challenging, but doing so with openness and honesty is vital. Approach the conversation with clear examples of actions that have triggered your concerns rather than accusations. This method fosters a constructive dialogue that invites your partner to respond with their perspective rather than putting them on the defensive.

Seeking professional help can also be a wise step in managing these delicate situations. Couples therapy, or individual therapy if your partner is not open to joint sessions, can provide a safe space to explore these issues. A therapist can help you unravel whether your fears are grounded in current relationship dynamics or echo past hurts and can offer strategies to address them. This professional guidance can be crucial in helping you navigate your feelings and the reality of your relationship without the bias of your anxious attachments.

Rebuilding trust after an incident of infidelity requires transparency, patience, and a commitment to healing from both partners. If you and your partner are dedicated to salvaging the relationship, establish a new foundation of honesty. That might mean more open communication about each other's thoughts, feelings, and daily experiences. Transparency about personal interactions, such as sharing details about one's day, can help rebuild the broken trust. Therapy can again play a crucial role here, providing tools and frameworks to guide this rebuilding process. Techniques such as developing a 'trust contract' where both partners explicitly state what behaviors are needed to rebuild trust can be part of this framework. Each small step toward transparency and consistency can help mend the fabric of trust that infidelity tears apart.

Moreover, it is crucial to work on rebuilding your self-esteem, whether the infidelity was real or perceived. Infidelity can shatter your self-worth, leaving you questioning your value and desirability. Engaging in activities that reinforce your sense of self, independent of your relationship, is vital. This can include reconnecting with hobbies, spending time with supportive friends, or setting personal goals. Building your self-esteem outside of your relationship can help you approach your partnership with more confidence and less fear, reducing the weight of anxious attachment.

Understanding the difference between perceived and actual infidelity is another important skill. Anxious attachment can sometimes blur these lines, making it feel like every unreturned call or friendly interaction your partner has is a potential threat. Educate yourself on the signs of genuine infidelity versus behaviors that are benign but trigger your anxieties. Discussing your thoughts with a trusted friend, family member, or therapist can provide a more objective perspective if you find it challenging to make these distinctions. They can help you see whether your fears are based on clear evidence or if they are more reflective of your insecurities. This differentiation is key in responding appropriately to your emotions and the realities of your relationship. It allows you to address genuine issues when they arise and soothe unwarranted fears rooted in anxious attachment.

Navigating the complexities of infidelity, particularly through the lens of anxious attachment, requires a balance of self-reflection, open communication, and professional support. By understanding the interplay between your attachment style and your relationship dynamics, you can approach these challenges with greater clarity and resilience, fostering a relationship environment where trust has the potential to flourish anew.

9.3 Anxious Attachment and Parenting Styles

Parenting, inherently a profound and transformative experience, often brings our deepest fears and strongest desires about attachment to the surface. For those among us grappling with anxious attachment, the way we interact with our children can unintentionally mirror the insecurities we harbor within ourselves. Understanding how anxious attachment styles can be transmitted from parents to children is pivotal. It isn't just behaviors that are passed down, but also patterns of emotional response and ways of connecting. When a parent displays constant anxiety about the stability of relationships, children can absorb these emotional cues and begin to view the world through a similar lens of insecurity. This cycle can perpetuate unless we actively seek to alter the course.

To disrupt this cycle, mindful parenting is an essential practice. It involves being present, not just physically but emotionally, tuning into your child's needs without letting your own anxieties dictate your response. For parents grappling with anxious attachment, one of the first steps is to recognize how this attachment style influences parenting behaviors. You might be overly worried about your child's safety or excessively sad during short separations. These reactions, while understandable, can send a message of instability to your child. By practicing mindfulness, you can start to separate your emotional responses from your child's actual needs, responding in a way that promotes security rather than projecting anxiety.

Adjusting parenting approaches to ensure that you provide a secure base involves creating an environment where your child feels consistently supported and loved, regardless of circumstances. This security allows children to explore the world confidently, knowing they have a safe emotional space to return to. For parents with anxious attachment, it's crucial to be aware of how your behaviors—such as clinging too tightly or needing constant reassurance from your child—can affect their perception of independence and security. Strategies like setting routines that give your child predictable, safe boundaries while allowing for exploration can be beneficial. Additionally, engaging in activities that build your own emotional resilience—such as therapy, meditation, or regular exercise—can help stabilize your internal environment, which in turn makes your emotional availability for your child more reliable and calm.

Balancing attachment and autonomy is a delicate dance. It's about fostering an emotional connection with your child that communicates love and availability without stifling their independence. Overprotection, a common pitfall for anxious attachers, can inhibit a child's ability to develop self-efficacy and resilience. To avoid this, encourage activities that promote your child's ability to operate independently. This could be as simple as letting them choose their clothes for the day or encouraging them to play independently with friends. Each step a child takes toward autonomy is an opportunity to reinforce their capability and resilience, qualities that they will carry into their own adult relationships. As you watch your child navigate these small challenges, offer support and guidance rather than stepping in to manage for them, thus promoting an internal sense of competence and security.

Coparenting plays a crucial role in managing anxious attachment effectively. Consistency between parents in terms of emotional response and caregiving strategies provides a stable, predictable environment that is essential for the child's secure attachment development. When both parents understand the implications of anxious attachment and work together to create a cohesive parenting approach, it significantly reduces the child's confusion and insecurity. Regular discussions with your coparent about strategies, expectations, and emotional challenges are important. These conversations can help align your parenting methods, ensuring both of you are contributing to a nurturing environment that promotes healthy attachment. It's also important to support each other's relationships with the child, recognizing that secure attachments with both parents are ideal for the child's emotional development.

Navigating parenting with an anxious attachment style isn't about achieving perfection. It's about striving for progress—recognizing and addressing your triggers, adjusting your behaviors, and consistently working toward providing a stable and loving environment for your child. By taking these steps, you not only enhance your child's emotional well-being but also embark on a path of healing and growth for yourself, transforming challenges into triumphs in the landscape of familial relationships.

9.4 The Influence of Cultural Differences on Attachment

Cultural perceptions of attachment vary widely across the globe, each bringing its unique influence to the relationships we forge. In some cultures, attachment is seen through a communal lens, where collective well-being supersedes the individual's needs, influencing individuals to form interdependent relationships. In contrast, other cultures prioritize independence and self-reliance, fostering a more individualistic approach to relationships. For someone with an anxious attachment style, these cultural frameworks can either exacerbate or alleviate their inherent anxieties. For instance, in a culture that values independence, an anxiously attached individual might struggle more intensely with fears of abandonment compared to within a culture where community support is readily available.

Navigating cross-cultural relationships introduces another layer of complexity. When partners hail from backgrounds with differing attachment norms, what one views as caring and involved, the other might see as clingy or overwhelming. This divergence can inadvertently heighten anxiety for someone already prone to anxious attachment, as they may constantly doubt the acceptability of their emotional expressions. It becomes essential to cultivate a deep understanding and respect for each other's cultural contexts. Open discussions about each partner's cultural expectations and norms regarding relationships can be enlightening. It's about creating a shared language for love—one that respects both cultural identities and fosters a secure middle ground where both partners can feel understood and valued.

Incorporating cultural sensitivity into therapeutic practices is crucial, especially when addressing issues related to attachment. Therapy, often grounded in Western ideals of individualism and self-exploration, may not resonate with individuals from cultures where collective harmony and familial obligations are paramount. Therapists must adapt their approach to honor these cultural values, ensuring that their therapeutic interventions do not inadvertently push clients toward behaviors that might feel alien or uncomfortable. For example, encouraging a client from a collectivist culture to set boundaries with family members must be handled with an understanding of the client's cultural emphasis on familial duty and respect. This culturally sensitive practice not only enhances the therapeutic relationship but also ensures that the healing process respects and integrates the individual's cultural identity, making it more meaningful and effective.

Global variations in attachment styles also provide a broader perspective on how different cultures approach relationships and attachment. Research shows significant differences in the prevalence of secure and insecure attachment styles across different countries and cultures. Understanding these variations is vital for anyone engaged in or working with cross-cultural relationships. It helps in setting realistic expectations and strategies for dealing with attachment-related challenges. For instance, knowing that a culture has a high prevalence of secure attachment styles might explain the general ease with which individuals form and maintain relationships and could be a reassuring factor for someone with an anxious attachment style entering a relationship in such a culture. Conversely, in cultures where insecure attachment styles are common, being aware of this can prepare an individual for potential challenges and encourage proactive strategies for building security and trust.

Navigating the complexities of attachment across different cultural landscapes requires flexibility, openness, and a willingness to learn and adapt. By embracing the rich tapestry of global cultural practices around attachment, individuals and therapists can better understand and address the unique challenges and opportunities these differences present. Whether it's through personal relationships or therapeutic interventions, broadening our understanding of global attachment practices enriches our interactions and enhances our capacity to build secure, fulfilling connections with others.

9.5 Managing Anxious Attachment in Alternative Relationships

In the rich tapestry of human relationships, diverse structures such as LGBTQIA+ identities, nonbinary individuals, polyamory, long-distance partnerships, and significant age-gap relationships present unique opportunities for growth and connection, especially for those experiencing anxious attachment. These relationships embrace a variety of expectations, creating a need for tailored strategies to foster security and trust amidst different styles of alternative frameworks, such as:

- **Pansexual:** Attracted to people regardless of their gender or gender identity. Pansexual individuals can be attracted to men, women, nonbinary people, and those who identify outside traditional gender norms.

- **Asexual:** Experiences little to no sexual attraction to anyone. Asexual individuals might still experience romantic attraction and engage in relationships without sexual activity.

- **Demisexual:** Experiences their sexual attraction after

forming a strong emotional connection with someone. Demisexual individuals typically do not feel sexual attraction towards strangers or casual acquaintances.

- **Sapiosexual:** Attracted to intelligence and intellectual conversations. Sapiosexual individuals find intellectual stimulation to be a primary factor in sexual attraction.

- **Queer:** A broad and inclusive term that covers various sexual orientations and gender identities outside the heterosexual and cisgender norms. It's used by individuals who don't fit into the traditional categories.

- **Skoliosexual:** Attracted to nonbinary people, those who do not identify strictly as male or female.

- **Androsexual:** Attracted to masculine gender presentation or men, regardless of the person's gender identity.

- **Gynosexual:** Attracted to feminine gender presentation or women, regardless of the person's gender identity.

For example, polyamory, where multiple consensual relationships coexist, can particularly amplify anxieties for someone prone to fears of abandonment and insecurity. The key to managing anxious attachment in such dynamics lies in forthright and frequent communication. It's crucial to establish clear agreements that respect all parties' boundaries and emotional needs. Regular relationship check-ins can be invaluable, offering a structured opportunity to reassess and adjust relationship dynamics, ensuring that everyone feels valued and heard. This open dialogue helps mitigate the insecurities that may arise from the complexities of loving multiple partners.

Long-distance relationships (LDRs) stretch the bond of trust and communication even further. The physical distance can trigger heightened anxieties for those with an anxious attachment style, often manifesting as a need for constant reassurance through calls or texts. To adapt attachment strategies effectively, LDR partners might benefit from setting clear expectations about communication frequencies and modalities. Establishing routines, such as good morning texts or weekly video calls, can create a rhythm of predictability that soothes anxious attachments, providing reassurance despite the miles of separation.

Relationships with significant age gaps can also introduce dynamics that may feel unsettling, especially if the younger partner harbors anxieties about long-term commitments and security. In such relationships, emphasizing transparency about each partner's needs and future expectations can prevent misalignments and anxieties from escalating. For instance, discussions about career trajectories, family planning, or retirement plans should be approached with openness and honesty, ensuring both partners feel secure in their shared path ahead.

Creating rituals and symbols of commitment can also play a crucial role in building security in these non-traditional relationships. Rituals, whether daily text updates or monthly day-long excursions, help in cementing a sense of continuity and presence. They act as tangible reminders of the relationship's solidity and the partners' commitment to each other. Similarly, symbols of commitment, such as shared playlists, custom jewelry, or even tattoos, can serve as everyday reminders of the bond and commitment, providing comfort and security to an anxiously attached individual.

Case Studies and Examples

Consider the story of Alex and Sam, a couple in a long-distance relationship. Alex, who has an anxious attachment style, initially struggled with overwhelming anxiety due to the physical distance. By establishing a ritual of nightly video calls and agreeing to send photos from their day, the couple created a sense of closeness and routine that helped mitigate Alex's anxieties. These simple acts of connection provided Alex with the reassurance needed to feel secure in the relationship.

In another instance, Jordan, who is polyamorous and nonbinary, found themselves feeling perpetually insecure in their relationships. By initiating regular relationship check-ins with their partners, Jordan was able to express their needs and fears without feeling burdensome. These discussions helped all involved to understand and address the underlying anxieties, reinforcing their commitment and adapting their behaviors to ensure everyone felt valued and secure.

These examples underscore the importance of tailored communication and commitment strategies in managing anxious attachment in alternative relationships. By proactively addressing the unique challenges these relationships present, individuals can foster a sense of security that supports healthy and fulfilling connections.

As we close this exploration of managing anxious attachment in non-traditional relationships, we see how adaptability, open communication, and personalized commitment rituals are crucial in navigating these complex dynamics. Each relationship structure, with its unique challenges, also offers unique opportunities for growth and deepening connections. As you move forward, may these insights empower you to cultivate security and joy in whatever form your relationships take.

Self-Assessment and Reflection Exercises for Chapter 9: Special Considerations in Anxious Attachment

1. Anxious Attachment in Digital Communication and Social Media:

- Exercise: Reflect on your recent digital communications. Identify any moments when you felt anxious or insecure. How did you respond? Write down a strategy from this chapter that you can use to manage these feelings in the future.

- Understanding how digital interactions can trigger anxious attachment and developing specific strategies to manage these feelings will help you use digital communication more healthily and securely.

2. Dealing with Infidelity and Anxious Reactions:

- Exercise: Think about a time when you felt insecure about your partner's commitment. What triggered these feelings, and how did you react? Discuss with your partner or write down how you can approach such situations differently using the strategies from this chapter.

- Reflecting on your reactions to perceived infidelity and learning to communicate openly about your concerns can help build trust and reduce anxiety in your relationship.

3. Anxious Attachment and Parenting Styles:

- Exercise: Identify moments when your anxious attachment style influenced your parenting. How did your reactions impact your child? Plan a strategy from this chapter to address similar situations more securely.

- Understanding how anxious attachment affects your parenting helps you develop more secure attachment behaviors with your children, fostering their emotional well-being and your confidence as a parent.

4. The Influence of Cultural Differences on Attachment:

- Exercise: Reflect on any cultural differences between you and your partner that have caused misunderstandings or anxiety. Write down how you can use strategies from this chapter to navigate these differences more effectively.

- Recognizing and addressing cultural differences with empathy and respect helps build stronger, more understanding relationships, reducing attachment-related anxieties.

5. Managing Anxious Attachment in Alternative Relationships:

- Exercise: Consider your experiences in non-traditional relationship structures (e.g., long-distance, polyamory). Identify any challenges related to your anxious attachment style. Plan how to implement strategies from this chapter to manage these challenges.

- Applying specific strategies for managing anxious attachment in alternative relationship structures helps you navigate these dynamics more securely and confidently, fostering healthier connections.

These exercises encourage self-reflection and the application of the strategies discussed in this chapter, helping you manage anxious attachment in various aspects of your life and relationships.

Chapter Ten

Empowering Your Journey Toward Secure Attachment

Imagine standing at the edge of a vast network of pathways, each trail interwoven with the stories and support of those who have walked before you. This network represents your support system, a fundamental element for anyone navigating the complexities of anxious attachment. Just as a tree relies on a robust root system to thrive in unpredictable weather, you too can cultivate a network of support that grounds and nourishes you through the storms of emotional upheaval. In this chapter, we explore how building a resilient support network can transform your journey toward secure attachment, providing a bedrock of emotional stability and continuous growth.

10.1 Building a Support Network for Emotional Resilience

Importance of a Supportive Community

The journey toward healing and secure attachment is seldom a solitary endeavor. It thrives on the nourishment provided by a supportive community. This network, comprising empathetic and understanding individuals, serves as a critical buffer against the inherent challenges of anxious attachment. Engaging with people who understand your struggles and provide emotional support can significantly enhance your resilience. They not only offer a shoulder to lean on during tough times but also celebrate your victories, reinforcing your progress and encouraging continued growth. The right community acts as a mirror, reflecting your worth and potential back to you, often reminding you of strengths you may overlook when isolated.

Steps to Build or Strengthen Your Support Network

Creating or strengthening your support network involves a proactive approach to connection. Begin by identifying groups that resonate with your experiences. This could be a local meetup of individuals interested in personal development or a more structured group focusing on mental health and attachment issues. Engaging with these communities allows you to form connections with individuals who share similar journeys. Furthermore, reach out to old friends who have shown understanding and compassion in the past. Rekindling these relationships can add valuable members to your support system.

Participating in community activities, whether they are directly related to mental health or broader interests like art classes or outdoor adventures, can also expand your network. These activities allow you to meet diverse individuals who can offer different perspectives and support as you navigate your path toward secure attachment. Each positive interaction within these groups reinforces your sense of belonging and support, crucial elements in building your emotional resilience.

Role of Support Groups and Therapy Groups

Support groups or therapy groups that focus on attachment issues provide a structured environment for sharing experiences and learning from others. These groups offer a unique platform where the nuances of attachment theories are not just discussed but deeply understood and empathized with. The collective wisdom of the group can offer new insights and strategies for managing your attachment style.

Facilitators in these groups often provide guided activities that enhance understanding and help in applying learning in real-world scenarios. This structured support is invaluable as it combines professional guidance with peer support, creating a dynamic environment conducive to healing and growth. Engaging regularly with such groups can significantly accelerate your journey toward understanding and adapting your attachment style in healthier ways.

Leveraging Online Communities

In today's digital age, geographical distance no longer needs to be a barrier to finding support. Online forums and social media groups dedicated to mental health and attachment issues can connect you with individuals across the globe who share your concerns and goals. These platforms offer a space to share stories, exchange resources, and offer help at times that are most convenient for you, making support accessible regardless of your location or schedule.

When engaging with online communities, it's important to maintain healthy boundaries and protect your privacy. Engage genuinely but cautiously, sharing your experiences while safeguarding your personal information. Additionally, be discerning about the advice you accept, cross-referencing suggestions with credible sources or professionals when necessary.

Textual Element: Interactive Element - Journaling Prompt

To actively engage with this chapter's theme, consider this journaling prompt: reflect on your current support system. Who are the individuals that offer you emotional support? Write about how each person contributes to your sense of security and emotional well-being. If your current network feels lacking, list the traits you seek in potential new members of your support network. How can you start forming connections with individuals who embody these traits? This exercise not only clarifies the current state of your support system but also sets a clear direction for how you can strengthen it.

By consciously building and nurturing your support network, you equip yourself with a vital toolkit for managing the ups and downs of anxious attachment. Remember, the strength of your support network often reflects the resilience with which you face life's challenges. As you expand and deepen your connections, you pave the way for a richer, more supportive journey toward secure attachment.

10.2 Continuing Education and Resources for Lifelong Attachment Health

Understanding your attachment style and its influence on your relationships is not a one-time task but a continuous journey that benefits immensely from ongoing education and the use of diverse resources. As you delve deeper into the nuances of attachment theory, you will see that this field is ever-evolving, with new insights and strategies emerging from current research. To truly nurture your attachment health, embracing a commitment to lifelong learning will equip you with the knowledge and tools necessary to adapt and grow through various life stages and relationship dynamics.

One of the most empowering steps you can take is to immerse yourself in the rich body of knowledge available on attachment theory. This can range from foundational texts like John Bowlby's seminal works on attachment to more contemporary analyses that explore the intersection of attachment with neurobiology, psychology, and interpersonal relationships. Academic journals and books are treasure troves of information, offering in-depth insights that can clarify complex concepts and introduce you to new ideas that resonate with your experiences. Moreover, online courses dedicated to psychological health and interpersonal relationships make this valuable information accessible to a wider audience, allowing you to learn at your own pace and convenience.

In addition to traditional educational resources, the digital age offers a plethora of multimedia tools that can enhance your understanding and engagement with attachment theory. Podcasts, for instance, provide a platform for therapists and experts to discuss attachment issues in a format that is both accessible and personal. Listening to these discussions can not only broaden your understanding but also introduce you to real-life scenarios and practical advice. Similarly, webinars and YouTube channels offer visual and interactive ways to connect with experts and community members who share your interest in improving relationship dynamics. These platforms often present information in a user-friendly manner, making complex concepts more understandable and relatable.

Participating in seminars and workshops presents a dual opportunity: to deepen your knowledge and to connect with professionals and peers who are also interested in attachment theory. These events often provide a more immersive experience, offering live demonstrations, interactive sessions, and the chance to ask questions directly to experts. The networking opportunities provided at such gatherings are invaluable, allowing you to build connections with others who can offer support, insights, and collaboration opportunities. These relationships can become part of your ongoing support network, providing mutual encouragement and sharing new resources and findings over time.

To ensure that your understanding of attachment theory remains current and relevant, it is crucial to regularly update yourself with the latest research and discussions in the field. This might involve subscribing to relevant publications, joining online forums where new studies and articles are discussed, or participating in community groups focused on psychological health. Staying informed about recent developments not only refreshes your knowledge but also inspires continuous personal growth and the application of new insights into your daily life and relationships.

By embracing these educational opportunities and resources, you empower yourself with a deeper understanding of your own behaviors and those of others. This ongoing commitment to learning and growth will enhance your personal development and enrich your relationships, allowing you to foster healthier, more fulfilling connections with those around you. As you continue to explore and apply the principles of attachment theory, remember that each step forward adds a valuable layer to your foundation of knowledge, supporting your path toward emotional well-being and secure attachments.

10.3 Celebrating Your Progress and Planning Next Steps

As you navigate through the evolving landscape of your attachment health, taking the time to pause and celebrate your progress is as vital as any step you take toward improvement. Recognizing and honoring the milestones you achieve, no matter their size serves as a powerful affirmation of your commitment to personal growth. This act of celebration will bolster your morale and fortify your resolve to continue advancing on this path.

When considering how to recognize these milestones, start by defining what constitutes a milestone for you. It could be as significant as reaching a year of therapy or as seemingly small as a week of no anxious episodes in your relationships. Each person's journey is unique, and thus, their milestones will be equally individual. Once you identify these achievements, think about how to celebrate them in ways that feel truly rewarding. This might involve a small personal ritual like a quiet evening with a favorite book or something more pronounced like a social gathering with close friends or supporters who have been part of your journey. The key is to make these celebrations resonate personally, reinforcing the positive changes you've made.

Setting future goals is also crucial to maintain momentum in your growth. Utilizing the SMART (Specific, Measurable, Achievable, Relevant, Time-bound) framework can immensely aid in this process. Begin by specifying what you want to accomplish. Be as precise as possible—vagueness can lead to goals that are difficult to measure and, consequently, harder to achieve. Ensure your goals are measurable; for instance, if improving communication is your aim, perhaps measure it by the number of open conversations you initiate each month. Your goals should be achievable; set realistic expectations that stretch your capabilities but remain within reach. Relevance is key—choose goals that truly matter to you and align with your broader objectives in life. Finally, set a timeline for these goals to maintain a sense of urgency and commitment.

Developing a comprehensive personal growth plan involves more than listing goals—it requires integrating strategies for maintaining secure attachments and preparing for potential setbacks. Incorporate daily or weekly practices that nurture your emotional health, such as mindfulness exercises or regular journaling. Also, devise a plan for coping with setbacks. This might include steps to take when feeling triggered, such as reaching out to a friend or engaging in a calming activity. Regular self-assessment is also crucial; set periodic reviews of your progress toward your goals and adjust your strategies as needed. This ongoing evaluation ensures that your growth plan remains dynamic and responsive to your changing needs and circumstances.

Embrace the notion that improving attachment health is a lifelong process. This perspective is not meant to be daunting but to remind you that growth is continuous and setbacks are natural parts of the learning curve. They provide invaluable opportunities to deepen your understanding of yourself and refine your strategies. Each challenge is a stepping stone, not a stumbling block, on your path to greater emotional resilience and healthier relationships.

As you reflect on the insights and strategies discussed in this chapter, remember that the progress you've made is a testament to your strength and commitment to bettering yourself and your relationships. The journey toward secure attachment might be lifelong, but each step you take is evidence of your resilience and capacity for growth. Carry forward the lessons learned, the milestones achieved, and the goals set as you continue to navigate the complexities of personal and relational development.

Self-Assessment and Reflection Exercises for Chapter 10: Empowering Your Journey Toward Secure Attachment

1. Reflecting on Personal Growth:

- Exercise: Think about your journey from the beginning of this book to now. Identify three significant changes or improvements you've made in your attachment style and relationships. Write a short paragraph for each change, explaining how you achieved it and how it has impacted your life.

This exercise helps you recognize and appreciate your progress, reinforces the positive changes, and builds confidence in your ability to continue growing.

2. Setting Future Goals:

- Exercise: Identify two specific areas where you still feel challenged in achieving a secure attachment. Set one short-term goal (to be achieved within the next month) and one long-term goal (to be achieved within the next six months) for each area. Write down actionable steps you will take to accomplish these goals.

- By setting concrete goals and outlining steps to achieve them, you create a clear roadmap for continued personal growth and development toward secure attachment.

3. Cultivating Self-Compassion:

- Exercise: Write a compassionate letter to yourself addressing your attachment struggles. Acknowledge your efforts and challenges, and offer yourself kindness and understanding. Reread this letter whenever you feel discouraged or overwhelmed.

- This exercise promotes self-compassion, crucial for maintaining resilience and motivation on your journey toward secure attachment.

4. Engaging with Your Support Network:

- Exercise: Reflect on how you've utilized your support network throughout your journey. Identify one person in your network who has been particularly supportive. Plan a way to express your gratitude to them, whether through a heartfelt conversation, a thank-you note, or a small gesture of appreciation.

- Acknowledging and appreciating your support network strengthens these relationships and reinforces the importance of seeking and valuing support.

5. Continuing Education:

- Exercise: Research and identify a new book, podcast, or course related to attachment theory or personal development that you have not yet explored. Commit to engaging with this new resource and set a date by which you will start and finish it.

- Engaging with new educational resources keeps you informed and inspired, providing ongoing opportunities for learning and growth.

These exercises are designed to foster deeper self-awareness, set clear goals for future growth, and strengthen your support system, all essential for continuing your journey toward secure attachment.

Conclusion

As we reach the conclusion of our journey together through the complexities yet wonderful differences of anxious attachment, it's important to pause and reflect on the ground we have covered. From uncovering the roots of anxious attachment in our earliest relationships to exploring the profound impact it can have on our adult interactions—whether romantic, platonic, or professional—we've delved into understanding this intricate style of connecting with others. We've armed ourselves with strategies not just for managing but for transforming anxious attachment into a more secure model, emphasizing the critical roles of self-awareness, open communication, diligent self-care, and an unwavering commitment to personal growth.

The essence of this book has been to illuminate the tangible possibility of change. The journey toward secure attachment, while challenging, is rich with opportunities for profound transformation. We've learned that through the power of self-reflection, mindfulness, and empathy, not only for others but crucially for ourselves, we can start to forge healthier and more fulfilling relationships. Building a robust support network and engaging with ongoing education about attachment theory are not merely suggestions but foundational steps toward a life where our relationships support and enrich us.

Remember, you hold the power to redefine your narrative. The anxious attachment styles shaped by past experiences need not set the blueprint for your future. Every chapter of your life offers a chance to forge a new path—one where understanding, patience, and consistent effort light the way to secure, loving connections.

Take the practical strategies and exercises that are peppered throughout this book and weave them into the fabric of your daily life. Consider engaging with therapy or support groups if you find yourself needing more structured guidance. Connect with others who are on similar paths and remember the strength found in shared experiences. Keeping a journal can also serve as a powerful tool to document your progress and reflect on any setbacks, viewing them as valuable lessons rather than defeats.

Setbacks are inevitable, as is the case with all worthwhile endeavors. When you encounter these moments, treat yourself and them with kindness, and see them as opportunities to deepen your understanding and refine your approach. Persistence, coupled with self-compassion and a willingness to seek help when necessary, will be your allies on this path.

Embarking on a journey of emotional growth and learning to develop a secure attachment style is a profound and transformative experience. This journey extends far beyond the realm of successful relationships; it's about the treasures you find within yourself as you evolve. As you cultivate a secure attachment style, you begin to flourish with confidence and certainty, not just in your relationships but in every aspect of your life.

Developing a secure attachment means recognizing and healing from past wounds, understanding your emotional patterns, and fostering self-compassion. It's about learning to trust yourself, embracing your worth, and becoming your own source of comfort and stability. This internal growth radiates outward, enriching your interactions and connections with others.

The true riches of this journey are found in who you become. As you develop a more secure attachment style, you build resilience, emotional intelligence, and a deeper sense of self. This foundation of confidence allows you to form healthier, more fulfilling relationships where mutual respect and understanding thrive.

Ultimately, the journey to secure attachment is a path of self-discovery and empowerment. You are unlocking your potential, embracing your authentic self, and creating a life filled with meaningful connections and unwavering self-assurance.

As you continue on your journey, stay curious about yourself and the dynamics of your relationships. Keep the doors of learning open and let your understanding of attachment theory evolve as you apply its principles across the different stages of your life. Lifelong learning is not just about personal enrichment—it's about continuously nurturing the health of your attachments.

To conclude, let me leave you with a message of hope and resilience. You are not alone in your struggles and the aspirations you hold for more secure and enriching relationships are within reach. With dedication, support, and a heart open to change, the path to healthier attachments is not just a possibility but a probable destination. Change is not only possible—it is waiting for you to embrace it. May your journey from here be filled with growth, healing, and the joy of deep, meaningful connections.

Thank you for allowing me to be a part of your journey toward understanding and healing. Here's to moving forward with courage and hope toward the greatest relationships of your life - and I wish for you a life you love living.

If you didn't find time earlier, would you take a moment to give my book your honest review now?

Dearest Reader,

As you know, Amazon's algorithm thrives on them. By leaving a review for this book, you'll be helping others discover it, which can help them feel the best they deserve to feel, too. Your review will make a significant difference for everyone.

It's very straightforward. Just click on this link to go straight to the review page: https://mybook.to/BmkN

Or scan the QR code with your phone if easier.

Thank you for your support!

Your 2 Bonus Gifts

The author crafted these transformational hypnosis tracks to help you relax, strengthen your self-esteem, and build confidence. These audio tracks will enhance the practical strategies you'll find throughout this book. We recommend you listen to them every day for at least 12 weeks to let the hypno-suggestions work their magic in your subconscious mind. They will strengthen over time with repeated use.

Whether you start your day or wind down at night, these tools are your allies in managing anxious attachment and embracing a healthier, more fulfilling life.

Bonus Gift 1: 8-Hour Sleep Transformation Track for Building Self-Esteem, Confidence, and Overcoming Anxious Attachment

Unlock a transformative night's rest with our exclusive 8-hour sleep hypnosis track designed with professionally crafted and carefully selected hypno-suggestions and affirmations to enhance your self-esteem and confidence while addressing anxious attachment challenges. This deeply relaxing audio guide will:

- Build a strong foundation of self-worth

- Instill a sense of inner confidence

- Promote a calm and peaceful mindset

- Encourage positive thinking patterns

- Aid in overcoming self-doubt and anxiety

- Reduce fears of abandonment and rejection

- Strengthen emotional resilience

- Foster a sense of secure attachment and trust

- Improve your ability to form and maintain healthy, fulfilling relationships

With this sleep hypnosis track, you can be confident that you're making a lasting investment in your personal growth, emotional strength, and better relationships.

Bonus Gift 2: 7-Minute Power Booster Track for Daily Confidence Boost and Emotional Stability

Need a quick pick-me-up during your day? The 7-minute power hypnosis track is designed to give you an instant boost of confidence and positivity while also helping to manage the effects of anxious attachment. This professionally designed, energizing audio session will:

- Instantly lift your mood

- Boost your confidence levels

- Enhance focus and clarity

- Reduce stress and anxiety

- Equip you with a positive mindset for any challenge

- Help maintain emotional equilibrium throughout the day

- Reinforce feelings of security and self-assuredness

- Enhance your interactions and build healthier relationships.

Use this quick track anytime you need a confidence boost, whether before a big meeting, a social event or to start your day on a high note. Feel great, empowered, and emotionally stable, and improve your relationships with this versatile, powerful tool.

How To Download

To access these incredible gifts, scan the QR code or click the link below and enter your name and email in the box. Once you do, you will automatically be sent access to them to download immediately. Don't miss this opportunity to enhance your journey and stay connected for more empowering resources in the future! Rest assured, your email will only be used for very occasional promotions, and we will never sell or misuse your information.

Use The link to Download Your Free Tracks:
https://www.xone.london/bonus-gifts
or Scan the QR Code

Take the next step in your journey to personal growth and transformation today!

Disclaimer: Please do not use the hypnosis or meditation tracks while driving, operating heavy machinery, or engaging in any activity that requires your full attention. These audio sessions are designed to induce deep relaxation and focus, impairing your ability to perform tasks requiring alertness. Use these tracks in a safe and comfortable environment where you can fully relax without distractions for optimal results and safety. Always consult a healthcare provider before beginning any new therapeutic or relaxation practice, especially if you have a medical or psychological condition.

About the author

Tanya, a distinguished professional with advanced qualifications including DHP(Adv), PGCert(Psychotherapy), Licensed NLP Practitioner, and Dip(Nutrition), among many others, is retiring and transitioning from nearly 25 years of a successful career in psychotherapy to a dynamic new chapter in transformation coaching, writing, and publishing. With a rich background as a full-time integrative psychotherapist, Tanya's career has spanned from running a thriving practice to lecturing across Europe. She was honored with a prestigious fellowship from the National Institute of Psychotherapists. Yet, her most rewarding accomplishment remains the countless lives she has transformed, guiding individuals toward healthier, happier futures.

Tanya's extensive experience and passion for empowerment drive her to blend deep expertise in psychotherapy with innovative coaching strategies. She supports individuals in overcoming challenges and unlocking their fullest potential.

In addition to her busy coaching practice, Tanya is an author and publisher of self-help materials. Her publications offer strategies for personal growth, emotional healing, and lasting positive change, serving as valuable resources for those on a journey of self-discovery and improvement.

Combining proven therapeutic methods with dynamic coaching techniques, Tanya provides clients and readers with effective tools for creating lasting positive change. Her passionate commitment to personal and professional growth continues to inspire, making her a sought-after coach and author for those ready to transform their lives.

In her spare time, Tanya enjoys walking and playing with her beloved dog and best friend, Boo. She finds peace and inspiration through meditation, walks in the forest, and enjoys exploring new ways to expand her mindfulness practice. An avid researcher, Tanya delves into various topics to fuel her creativity, whether writing, developing new coaching strategies, or engaging in artistic projects, but most of all, she loves creating the life she loves living.

References

American Psychological Association. (n.d.). The origins of attachment theory: John Bowlby and Mary Ainsworth. Retrieved from https://psycnet.apa.org/record/1993-01038-001

American Psychological Association. (n.d.). Building your resilience. Retrieved from https://www.apa.org/topics/resilience/building-your-resilience

Attachment Project. (n.d.). Anxious attachment style guide: Causes & symptoms. Retrieved from https://www.attachmentproject.com/blog/anxious-attachment/

Attachment Project. (n.d.). Attachment repair group. Retrieved from https://www.attachmentproject.com/attachment-repair-groups/#:~:text=Group%20processes%20have%20been%20shown,also%20be%20healed%20through%20relationships

Attachment Project. (n.d.). Attachment-based goals for relationships that last. Retrieved from https://www.attachmentproject.com/blog/attachment-based-goals-for-relationships-that-last/

Attachment Project. (n.d.). How to self-soothe anxious attachment triggers. Retrieved from https://www.attachmentproject.com/blog/self-regulation-anxious-attachment-triggers/

Attachment Project. (n.d.). Setting limits: Boundaries and attachment styles. Retrieved from https://www.attachmentproject.com/blog/boundaries-and-attachment-styles/

Calmerry. (n.d.). How to get over a fear of rejection – 10 effective steps. Retrieved from https://calmerry.com/blog/anxiety/10-steps-to-get-over-your-fear-of-rejection/

Calmer You. (n.d.). How to self-soothe anxious attachment. Retrieved from https://www.calmer-you.com/how-to-self-soothe-anxious-attachment/

Columbia Psychiatry. (n.d.). How attachment styles influence romantic relationships. Retrieved from https://www.columbiapsychiatry.org/news/how-attachment-styles-influence-romantic-relationships

Dawn Health. (n.d.). How to cope and communicate with your partner. Retrieved from https://www.dawn.health/blog/anxiety-and-relationships-how-to-cope-and-communicate-with-your-partner

Everyday Speech. (n.d.). Empathy: A cornerstone of effective communication and connection. Retrieved from https://everydayspeech.com/blog-posts/general/empathy-a-cornerstone-of-effective-communication-and-connection/

Gottman Institute. (n.d.). How to build trust with your partner after infidelity. Retrieved from https://www.gottman.com/blog/how-to-build-trust-with-your-partner-after-infidelity/

Gottman Institute. (n.d.). How to use mindfulness to strengthen your relationships. Retrieved from https://www.gottman.com/blog/how-to-use-mindfulness-to-strengthen-your-relationships/

Healthline. (n.d.). Anxious attachment: Signs in children and adults, causes, and management. Retrieved from https://www.healthline.com/health/mental-health/anxious-attachment

JC Therapy. (n.d.). Differences between psychodynamic psychotherapy and CBT. Retrieved from https://jc-therapy.com/comp-cbt/

Medcalf, A. (n.d.). Empathy in relationships is the key to connection and communication. Retrieved from https://abbymedcalf.com/empathy-in-relationships-is-the-key-to-connection-and-communication/

Medium. (n.d.). How to successfully work through all types of conflict in relationships. Retrieved from https://medium.com/adam-rebecca-murauskas/how-to-successfully-work-through-all-types-of-conflict-in-relationships-87314f37eef

Mind Tools. (n.d.). How to write SMART goals, with examples. Retrieved from https://www.mindtools.com/a4wo118/smart-goals

National Center for Biotechnology Information. (2016). Disorganized attachment and personality functioning in adulthood. Retrieved from https://www.ncbi.nlm.nih.gov/pmc/articles/PMC5026862/

National Center for Biotechnology Information. (2017). From the cradle to the grave: The effect of adverse childhood experiences on adult health outcomes. Retrieved from https://www.ncbi.nlm.nih.gov/pmc/articles/PMC5600283/

National Center for Biotechnology Information. (2017). Manifestation of trauma: The effect of early traumatic experiences on brain function. Retrieved from https://www.ncbi.nlm.nih.gov/pmc/articles/PMC5364177/

National Center for Biotechnology Information. (2020). Culture and child attachment patterns: A behavioral genetics approach. Retrieved from https://www.ncbi.nlm.nih.gov/pmc/articles/PMC6901642/

National Center for Biotechnology Information. (2021). A lifespan development theory of insecure attachment. Retrieved from https://www.ncbi.nlm.nih.gov/pmc/articles/PMC8469853/

National Center for Biotechnology Information. (2021). Neural basis underlying the trait of attachment anxiety and the importance of the ventromedial prefrontal cortex in the modulation of threat: An fMRI study. Retrieved from https://www.ncbi.nlm.nih.gov/pmc/articles/PMC7901076/

National Center for Biotechnology Information. (2022). Relationship between social media use and attachment styles. Retrieved from https://www.ncbi.nlm.nih.gov/pmc/articles/PMC9966679/

National Center for Biotechnology Information. (2023). Exploring the association between attachment style, relationship satisfaction, and mental health outcomes. Retrieved from https://www.ncbi.nlm.nih.gov/pmc/articles/PMC10047625/

National Institute of Mental Health. (n.d.). Caring for your mental health. Retrieved from https://www.nimh.nih.gov/health/topics/caring-for-your-mental-health

Positive Psychology. (n.d.). 7 most effective self-esteem tools and activities. Retrieved from https://positivepsychology.com/self-esteem-tools-activities/

Positive Psychology. (n.d.). 7 ways to improve communication in relationships. Retrieved from https://positivepsychology.com/communication-in-relationships/

Positive Psychology. (n.d.). 8 powerful self-compassion exercises & worksheets. Retrieved from https://positivepsychology.com/self-compassion-exercises-worksheets/

Psych Central. (n.d.). 21 ways to increase intimacy and communication with an avoidant partner. Retrieved from https://psychcentral.com/relationships/ways-to-increase-intimacy-and-communication-with-an-avoidant-partner

Psychology Today. (2017). When childhood trauma meets healing relationships. Retrieved from https://www.psychologytoday.com/us/blog/call/201703/when-childhood-trauma-meets-healing-relationships

Psychology Today. (2019). The right way to negotiate with your partner. Retrieved from https://www.psychologytoday.com/us/blog/marriage-equals/201902/the-right-way-negotiate-your-partner

Psychology Today. (n.d.). Finding an attachment-based therapist. Retrieved from https://www.psychologytoday.com/us/blog/the-freedom-change/202102/finding-attachment-based-therapist

Thomas Blake Therapy. (n.d.). Unlocking healing: The success of EMDR therapy. Retrieved from https://www.thomasblaketherapy.com/blog/unlocking-healing-the-success-of-emdr-therapy

Verywell Mind. (n.d.). Attachment therapy: Definition, techniques, and efficacy. Retrieved from https://www.verywellmind.com/attachment-therapy-definition-techniques-and-efficacy-5203776

Verywell Mind. (n.d.). Journaling for anxiety relief. Retrieved from https://www.verywellmind.com/journaling-a-great-tool-for-coping-with-anxiety-3144672

Milton Keynes UK
Ingram Content Group UK Ltd.
UKHW020311021124
450424UK00013B/1189